Stage Lighting Revealed

Stage Lighting Revealed

A Design and Execution Handbook

Glen Cunningham

WAVELAND

PRESS, INC.

Long Grove, Illinois

For information about this book, contact:
Waveland Press, Inc.
4180 IL Route 83, Suite 101
Long Grove, IL 60047-9580
(847) 634-0081
info@waveland.com
www.waveland.com

To Anne, Teren, and Kevin with all my love.

Foreword

This book is the result of years of coming up against a lack of information about stage lighting in a readily available form. From my beginning theater days in high school, through years as a professional technician, into working in sales and engineering for a major stage lighting manufacturer, I have run into the fact that there is little information available on how to mount a show's lighting.

Upon coming to work for Lighting & Electronics, I learned of a dream of the founder, James Fedigan. He wanted to create a small handbook of lighting to get information on how to use stage lighting equipment to the people who wished to learn. Remembering my early searches, listening to people I have had work for

me over the years, answering L&E's customers' questions, and thinking about the ideas Mr. Fedigan had about answering those questions in an easily used form helped me decide to write this book. Though James Fedigan passed away before the book began to be written, it was his dream that got me started. In that way he has been a part of providing the information so many people requested.

I hope this book will help someone get started in setting up the lights of performances in a more relaxed and rewarding atmosphere than many of us did in the past. Taking the information presented here and building on it through experience and experimentation should lead to a successful pastime, if not a career.

Contents

Introduction

A slow ballad plays, with the stage bathed in a dim indigo wash of light. The soloist stands at the center of the stage spotted in white light coming from a steep angle, effectively isolating him from the rest of the stage. A faint red wash from his right indicates early dawn. The audience is captured in a feeling of quiet intimacy. The soloist is the object of their complete focus. They are alone together, without the company of even those sitting next to them. The song ends and they are held in a dark limbo for a moment, making their individual world complete in the darkness. After a moment a single drumbeat sounds, and BANG! The stage explodes with bright ambers, reds, and oranges. The stage becomes so intense it seems to float up before them. It is party time and the entire audience is involved. From intimate to exuberant in a single beat.

Lighting can create an infinite number of dramatic effects. Varying color and intensity can produce a full range of moods from calm to excited, sad to exhilarated. No other medium can establish a mood more effectively than lighting. Dramatic examples of how effectively lighting can set the mood of a scene occur at any concert or theatrical production with a good lighting design.

Lighting can also create some very realistic effects, the setting of time being the most common. With the proper choice of colors and intensities, sunrise, bright afternoon, and stormy evening can be presented. Effective lighting completes both the emotional and the literal portrayals of any performance piece, accenting words, music, and movement.

The information in this book is presented in much the same order as it is used when creating or executing a lighting design. To create an effective design you must first understand the basic functions of lighting and the qualities of light used to carry out these functions. Next, you should decide what you want to create, or say, with your lighting; lay out the visual messages you wish to convey. Then it is time to determine how the design can be executed. This book is concerned with the design and execution of lighting for the performed piece today. Therefore, there is no discussion of the history of stage lighting and stage lighting fixtures.

To take a design and bring it to reality requires an understanding of the equipment and the process of mounting the lighting for a show. Lighting is a blend of aesthetic and technical creation. The visualization of what is to happen is an abstract process, a series of wishes and dreams. The execution of a design is the nuts-and-bolts phase of the process. By addressing both the aesthetic and technical aspects of lighting design this book attempts to set aside much of the mystery of stage lighting and reveal the underlying practices that allow and stimulate creative expression.

One intention of this book is to offer an introduction to stage lighting design, showing some of the different aims and processes involved in the creation of a design. There are more theories about what stage lighting design is and what it is supposed to do than there are lighting designers. Most of them are quite sound and very workable. The processes and techniques detailed throughout this book are only examples of the multitude of choices available to you. The book's purpose is to get you started on your own journey, not to be your final destination. Throughout the text it is suggested that you experiment whenever possible. By doing so you will develop your own style and repertoire of techniques. Whatever methods you choose to follow to create a design, strive to understand the functions of light in order to achieve the greatest complement to the performance possible. Make a point of watching techniques used in stage plays, concerts, and music videos. By watching carefully you can see examples of effective and ineffective lighting. This process is not very different from watching a musician to learn some good riffs.

Another objective of this book is to give the stage lighting designer and technician information concerning the equipment used and procedures often followed when lighting a show. Descriptions of various pieces of equipment and common practices used in stage lighting are given. If your interest is in executing a design of either your own or someone else's creation, you should have an understanding of what is required of the lighting as well as an understanding of the equipment you will be using. Someone who understands only the *mechanics* of stage electrics without regard to the *function* of stage lighting will not be able to finesse a show as well as someone who has a solid understanding of both.

As a designer or an electrician, create original interpretations of a performance with light. New lighting techniques are rare and generally occur naturally within the process of interpreting what needs to be lit.

An effective lighting design is like a beautiful painting. Your medium is bringing someone to an emotional state he or she would not achieve at that moment without your art. This does not and can not happen by accident. Don't shortchange yourself and just throw up lights and bump whatever colors are on hand up and down. Think about what you are trying to achieve. You will have a better time, the performers' show will be enhanced, and the audience will have a more fulfilling experience. Everyone wins.

PART I
Lighting Design

The Functions of Light

Successful lighting is the result of fulfilling the functions of lighting while supporting and enhancing the performance being lit. This is done by taking advantage of the qualities of lighting that achieve those functions. Once you are comfortable with the functions of lighting and how you go about fulfilling them, you will find it natural to use this understanding when beginning the process of creating a lighting design. Whether it happens consciously or not, achieving these functions must take place for the lighting of a performance to work.

THE FUNCTIONS OF LIGHTING

The four functions of lighting are visibility, reinforcement, composition, and mood.

Visibility

Visibility is the full range of seeing. What is not visible is as much a function of lighting as what is visible. Visibility is generally considered the primary function of lighting.

Reinforcement

Reinforcement means giving reason to the scene. Whether the desired effect is abstract or realistic, the lighting must justify and support it. For example, a dark, midnight blue wash would not support a bright afternoon scene, whereas bright, full stage lighting with hints of pinks and ambers would.

Composition

Composition is defining objects or areas of the scene in relation to their importance to the scene. The center of action should be the focus of the lighting instead of those areas not involved with the scene. A doorway lit brighter than the rest of the scene will distract from the action by leading the audience to expect an important entrance is about to take place.

Mood

Mood is the feeling or tone conveyed within a scene. A dark stage washed in blues and violets can set up a feeling of mystery.

THE QUALITIES OF LIGHT

The qualities of light that help achieve the above functions are:

- Intensity — the range of brightness used in a scene.
- Color — the range of hues and tints chosen to modify the light projected.
- Form — the variety and contrasts in both intensity and color used throughout a scene.
- Movement — any change in intensity, color, or form directing attention to a desired place.

The means for creating the above qualities of lighting are:

- Position — the location of the lighting instruments in relation to the objects or areas being lit.
- Equipment — the types of lighting instruments, lamps, color media, control, and cabling required to achieve the desired effects.

HOW THE EYE WORKS

When a designer is faced with the task of creating a variety of effects, it can be helpful to have a basic understanding of how the human eye reacts to light. Light entering the eye first passes through a clear membrane called the cornea. It then passes through the iris. The iris controls the amount of light that passes into the eye. It does this by enlarging, or dilating, to allow more light in under darker conditions, and by constricting, or shrinking, to limit the amount of light that passes under brighter conditions. The process of dilating and constricting is called *adaptation*. Something that should be considered when lighting a stage is that the process of adapting to changing light levels, from dark to light and light to dark, can take several moments. Adjusting from a very bright situation to a very dark one, called *dark adaptation*, can take longer than half an hour. If a shift in the lighting goes very rapidly from a very bright stage to a very dark one, people may have a hard time seeing what is on stage. This can be an advantage and a disadvantage. If you are trying to hide a scene change for instance, a blackout from a brightly lit stage could keep the audience temporarily blinded long enough to mask the change. If, however, a bright scene is immediately followed by a fast fade to a dark one, the audience could easily miss some important action on the stage while their eyes are trying to adjust.

The opposite change in light levels, from dark to light, is called *light adaptation*. Light adaptation most often takes just a few moments. It should be understood, however, that extreme changes from dark to light can be uncomfortable for the audience and in some cases cause a degree of pain. Another form of adaptation that should be understood is called *transient adaptation*. This is when the viewer is forced to look from an area of one light level to one of a higher or lower level. The result is that the eye has trouble adjusting properly, and either the lighter area appears too bright or the darker area appears too dark. The eye will generally adjust to the brightest area to protect itself from damage. When most of the viewing area is dark with only a small area of brightness, the eye tends to undercompensate for the bright area, washing that area out a bit. The process of transient adaptation can be used to your advantage if you wish to hide an area of the stage. Keeping that area considerably darker than the rest can make it appear black to the audience, effectively masking the area off from inquisitive eyes.

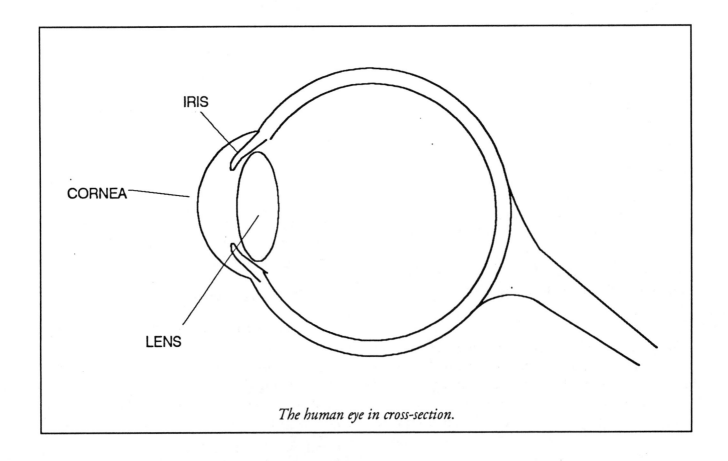

The human eye in cross-section.

Design Development

FIND THE EMOTIONAL CONTENT

When beginning the process of relating the lighting to the piece being lit, first determine the literal requirements of the piece, such as morning light, sunset, moonlight. After these are known and the level of realism required is agreed upon, you should look at the emotional rather than the literal content of the piece. This is the key to your lighting. Most performances bring the audience on some kind of emotional journey. Your lighting should complement these emotions so that a person watching will experience the same emotions as a person listening to or reading the piece but at a heightened level. The piece must be broken down into its emotional moments so that you can create an individual scene for each. Look at these moments and determine how the functions or qualities of light would help present them.

Is the moment a high or low emotion, full of energy or subdued? Everything has to be taken into account for the lighting to work with the piece. A cool stage (blues, greens, violets) can create a calm feeling. If the scene is trying to get everyone excited, you would be working against the scene to cast it in a dim blue wash. A warm stage (ambers, yellows, reds) has more excitement and energy to it. If the intensities are bright, the entire stage is involved; low level lighting tends to focus the audience's attention more on whoever is highlighted and creates a more somber atmosphere. Color and light levels are effectively used in presenting bold contrasts as well as subtle hints. A bright stage, apparently lit with white light, can give the feel of a cold winter day if there is actually a barely perceptible level of blue in the lighting.

You should experiment with different looks on stage to see what moods and effects are created. If you wish to direct the audience's attention to a new position but not change the entire scene, change the color or intensity of that area (the quality of movement), and

their eyes will be attracted to that place. This control can be done very subtly, with no one consciously aware of the visual directions he or she is receiving.

AVOID THE "TOO MUCH, TOO SOON" SYNDROME

One common mistake designers can make is to use too many effects too soon. This means that you should hold some of your ideas back, using them to give a different look to scenes occurring later in the performance. If you throw every look into the first few scenes, the rest of the show's lighting will seem commonplace and become boring. Also, be sure to give the lighting room to build with the action. If the scene starts out slow or quiet be sure your lighting conveys the same feeling. This way if the scene builds in energy or suspense you will be able to reinforce it with your light, building up with the scene.

During one production the director made some very interesting choices for the presentation of the show's climactic ballad. The song began with a singer on stage presenting a beautifully personal and intimate performance. As the song progressed, building in energy, a couple entered, carrying the song through to an energy-charged climax. This could have been an incredibly dramatic performance if the settings and lighting had been able to support the performance character. Instead, the scene opened with full stage lighting, a larger than life setting, and broad choreography. The intimacy of the performance's opening was lost, and the building of energy throughout the song seemed less pronounced since the settings and lighting had nowhere to go with the performance. Focus was nearly lacking altogether. Reinforcement is a very important and effective function of lighting. It not only applies to the time of day or the weather in a scene, it also applies to the general mood and energy level of the scene.

A roughed-in light sketch to help illustrate a moment in the show.

DETERMINE WHAT TO HIGHLIGHT

Once you determine the basic feel you want the lights to create, you have to determine what or who is going to be highlighted on the stage, if it is necessary to do so. This is often done by spotting that object or person with white or pale-colored light. The intensity depends on the intensity of the rest of the stage.

After each picture is created you will have to determine how you wish to connect these moments. This, too, should be taken from the performance. Do the moments jump one right into the other? Then the light scenes should also. If they meld one into the other, then the light scenes should fade from one to the next.

IMPORTANT PREPARATION

A clear and complete idea of what the lighting should look like and do should be laid out before the equipment needed is even considered. Too often designers get caught up in the technical aspects of lighting design before these aspects should be addressed. This only serves to limit and sometimes block the creative process of designing. It is very common for people to view the light plot as the lighting design, but this is very far from the truth. The creation of the look of the lighting is the lighting *design*; the light plot is merely an engineered map or schematic, a working drawing of how to build the design.

Sketching Roughs

When possible, a good practice is to create sketches of the lighting scenes in your design. These are rough renderings of the stage with focus on the lighting instead of the settings. It is considered mandatory for scene designers to render their designs before creating shop drawings for them, and the same is true of costume designers. It is rare, however, to see a sketch or rendering illustrating a lighting moment for a performance piece.

Color

Earlier in the book it was mentioned that colors and brightness levels have fairly predictable emotional effects on most people. Cool colors, such as greens and blues, tend to be very restful and refreshing. Warm colors like ambers, yellows, and pinks are more uplifting. Warmer colors still, such as reds and oranges, are more exciting. Bright stages create energy; dark stages create a more reflective mood. Experimentation is the key to understanding these different effects.

THE PRIMARY COLORS OF LIGHT

The primary colors in light are red, blue, and green. Combining all three primaries creates white light. Combining two primaries creates secondary colors: yellow (red and green), cyan (green and blue), and magenta (blue and red). If you were to combine a primary with the secondary color that results from mixing the other two primaries, you would again obtain white light. Thousands of hues and tints may be created by combining different amounts of the primary or secondary colors.

USING GEL TO ACHIEVE COLOR EFFECTS

The process of choosing and then achieving the desired color with combinations of the primaries can be difficult and time-consuming. Fortunately, the task has been greatly simplified by the use of plastic gel, available in hundreds of different hues, tints, and color temperatures (see the section on lamps for more information on color temperature). The most commonly used gels are Lee Filters, Roscolux, and Roscolene. Lee Filters and Roscolux are both capable of withstanding high temperatures, while Roscolene (although slightly less expensive) tends to burn through more quickly. Sheets of Lee are 21" x 24"; Roscolux and Roscolene are 20" x 24". You can get six 7 ½" x 7 ½" gel cuts or four 10" x 10" cuts from a sheet of gel. Most companies that supply gel offer swatch books containing samples of all the different colors available in a particular type; specify Lee Filters, Roscolux, or Roscolene. (See Appendix 6 for a gel reference and comparison chart.)

The greater the amount of primary color in a particular color, the more *saturated* it is said to be. (The inclusion of white, generated by the three primaries in equal amounts, creates a paler tint.) Generally, saturated colors are used only for stage washes and for *effect* lighting (any lighting not used primarily for visibility). Gel in saturated colors tends to burn more quickly than unsaturated gel colors do, particularly in blues and greens.

One way to get a larger variety of "looks" with minimal instrumentation and dimming is to change some gel colors between acts or sets. This helps avoid the constant repetition of the same few looks.

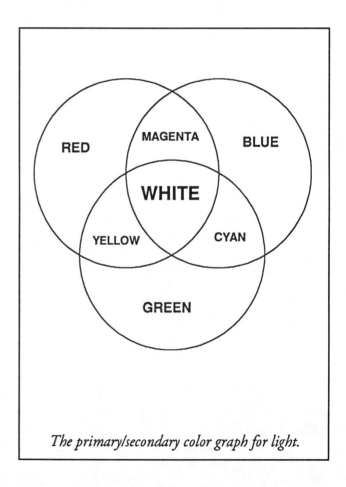

The primary/secondary color graph for light.

Lighting Positions

This is probably a good place to explain stage directions. All stage directions are given from the point of view of an actor standing in the center of the stage (center stage or CS), facing the audience. This person's left is stage left (SL), his right is stage right (SR). Now picture the stage slanted (raked), with the back wall higher than the front of the stage near the audience. (This is how stages used to be built.) An actor walking away from the audience would be walking up the stage, now referred to as upstage (US); walking toward the audience would be walking down the stage, now termed downstage (DS). The audience seating area is referred to as the house; therefore any lighting positions out over the audience are called *house positions*.

Where the light comes from plays an important part in what it does for the picture you wish to create. Some effects can only be created by light coming from one or two directions. If it is poorly planned, light from some directions will destroy the mood you are trying to create. There are five basic lighting positions to work with: Front, Side, Back, Down, and Background (or Cyc — named for the cyclorama, a drop that helps create the illusion of infinite space). You should understand that the angles of projection given in the following descriptions are for guidance only. At times you will want to — or, due to the theater architecture, have to — use angles other than those given.

FRONT LIGHTING

Front lighting is generally used for visibility and color washes. The lights used to make the performers visible are often gelled in pale colors (or no color). It is best if these lights shine down from about 30° to 50° off horizontal. Steeper angles, above 50°, create harsh shadows on faces. Shallower angles, below 30°, tend to flatten out features, particularly facial features. Lighting intended for color washes from the front, generally utilizing darker colors, is usually projected from shallow angles of 20° to 30°. Front lighting used to highlight a particular person or object (a light *special*)

is used at a steeper angle of 50° to 80° to create isolation. Front lighting coming up from a low angle can create an eerie feeling similar to the effect used in horror movies of the 1940s. General front lighting is most often brought in from angles off to one side or the other at approximately 45° from full front. This enables two different colors or intensities to be brought in from opposite sides to model (shape with light and shadow) the subject being lit and to create a sense of depth. Fixtures commonly used for front lighting are ellipsoidals (front of house and on stage), fresnels (usually only on stage), and PAR's (usually on stage, sometimes front of house).

SIDE LIGHTING

Side lighting is generally used for effect lighting. Side lighting creates more extreme modeling and accents arm and leg movement. Side lighting is particularly dramatic when used with bold colors, often with contrasting colors coming from opposite sides of the stage. Side lighting coming in at shallow angles sweeps the stage with minimal instrumentation, whereas steeper angles isolate smaller areas covered by each instrument and can throw across stage without lighting closer objects. You will commonly find ellipsoidals or PAR's used for side lighting, though occasionally fresnels and striplights are used also.

BACK LIGHTING

Back lighting is also effect lighting. It is one of the most popular positions used in concert lighting, mainly due to the fact that back light instruments are more visible to the audience and become a strong part of the setting. Back lighting creates a halo effect on the performers' heads and shoulders. Back lighting also helps create a sense of depth on stage. Coming up from a low angle, back lighting can help create a beautiful silhouette. Strong colors are often used in back lighting. When positioning back light, you should consider the people in the audience. It can be extremely

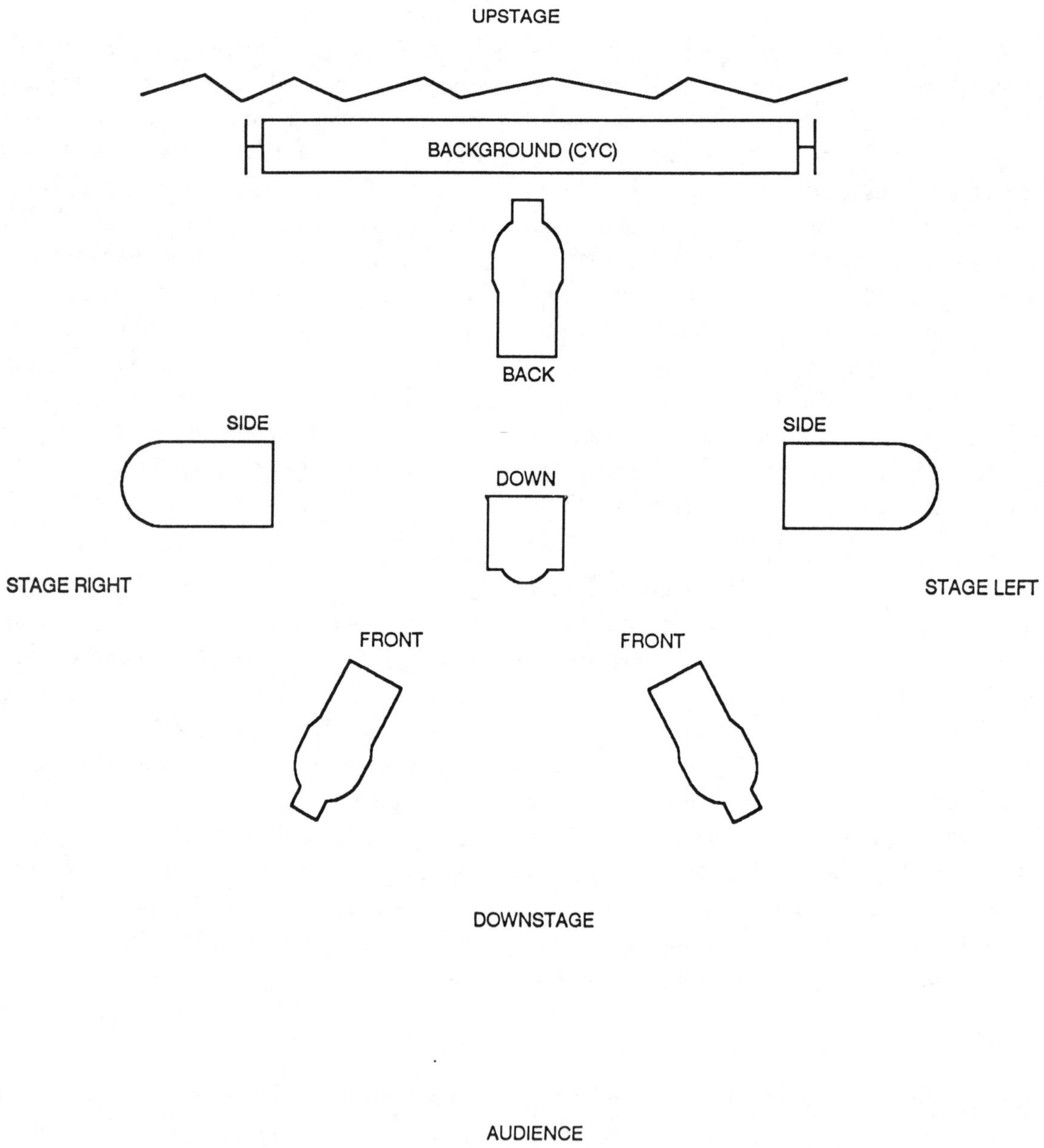

UPSTAGE

BACKGROUND (CYC)

BACK

SIDE

DOWN

SIDE

STAGE RIGHT

STAGE LEFT

FRONT

FRONT

DOWNSTAGE

AUDIENCE

A floor plan view of stage directions and lighting positions.

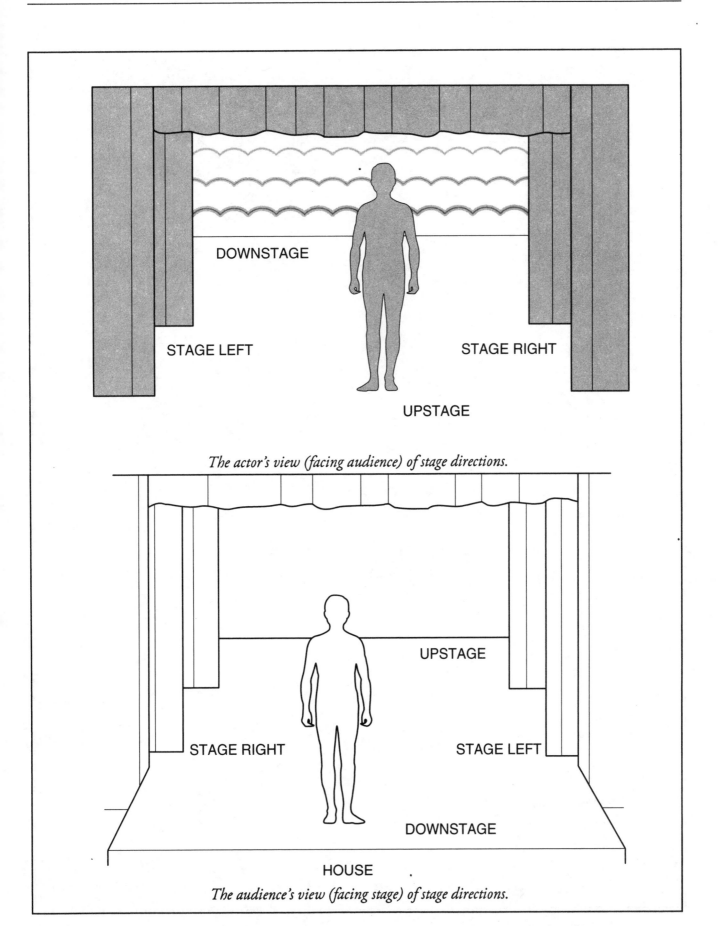

The actor's view (facing audience) of stage directions.

The audience's view (facing stage) of stage directions.

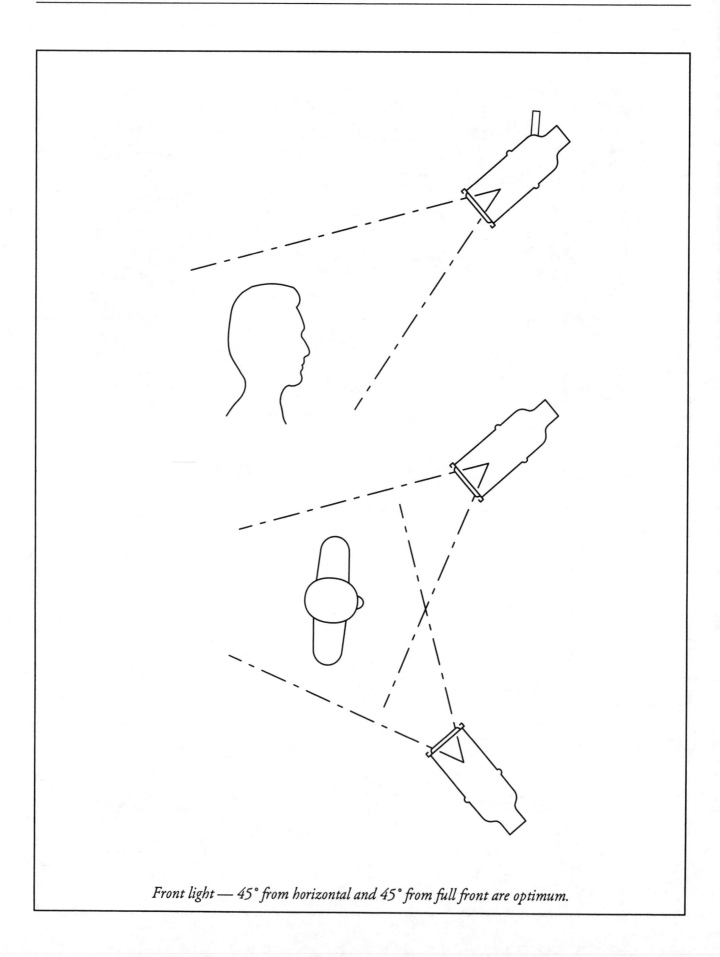

Front light — 45° from horizontal and 45° from full front are optimum.

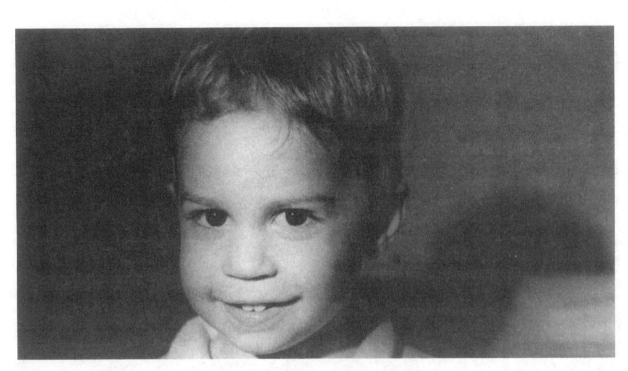

Front light with a single light source.

uncomfortable to look directly into a lighting instrument throughout an entire show. If that is not the mood you wish to create, you should keep your back lighting at a steep enough angle that it stays out of people's eyes. PAR's, fresnels, and occasionally ellipsoidals are most often used for back lighting.

DOWN LIGHTS

Down lights are good for highlighting specials or for color fills. Down lights are often used to draw attention to one person or to one particular action on stage. Down lighting can also be used to create the illusion of depth. A down light wash can effectively separate one person from the others on stage. It can also provide visibility for the musician trying to read his or her music on a music stand. PAR's, fresnels, and at times ellipsoidals are used as down lights.

BACKGROUND LIGHTING

Background lighting (or cyc lighting) is extremely powerful in creating a picture. If it is brighter and

bolder than the rest of the stage, it can overpower the rest of the scene. Colors are generally chosen to accent the foreground with deeper colors and lower intensities. Cyc lighting can create an extremely beautiful and dramatic silhouette on stage. Most often striplights of some design are used for background lighting. Scoops are also sometimes used.

EXPERIMENT WITH LIGHTING

Experiment with moving one light around a person to see the effect each position has on his or her face. Any light source will do, including a table lamp in your home. Just try to use one that is fairly concentrated in its focus so its effect will be dramatic. Add a second light and try it again. Once you see what the various positions do, you will become more comfortable using them.

Side light.

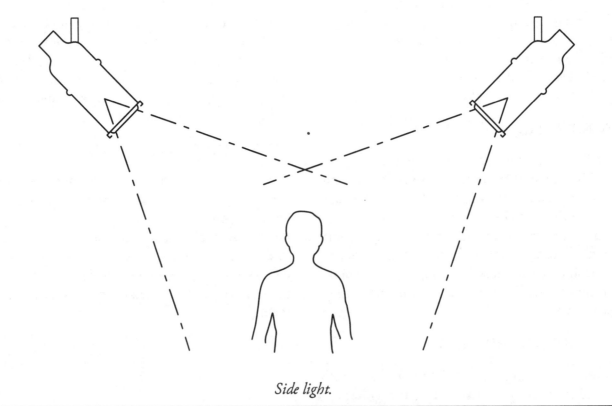

Side light.

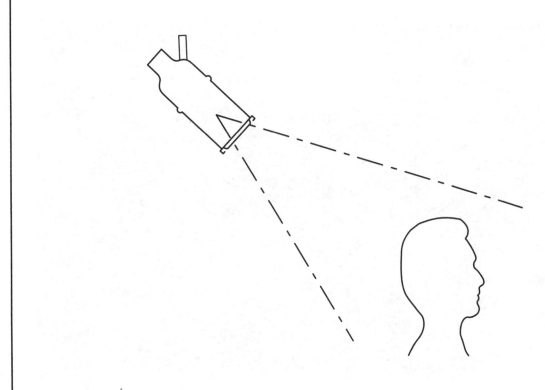

Back light.

Back light.

Down light.

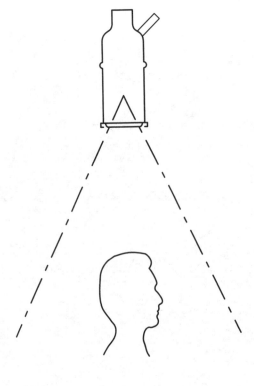

Down light.

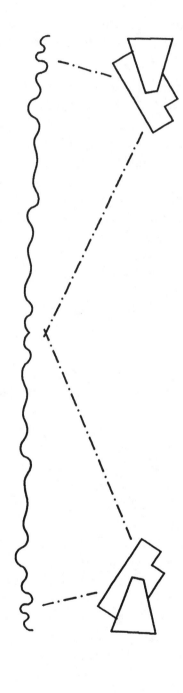

Background, or cyc, light.   *Background light (from below).*

Design Layout

After the design is created and the look of the stage is finalized, it is time to begin the process of laying out the design. This is the point where you have to translate your aesthetic descriptions of a cold or hot stage, a wild splash of color, a murky morning into actual, definable lighting effects. Every designer has a different approach to laying out the design. For some it begins at the very early stages of design. Others prefer to define the visual imagery they wish to create before getting involved in the logistics of executing the design. Whichever approach is used, the same questions are raised no matter what kind of performance is being lit. It is just a matter of when the questions are addressed and how.

The following breakdown of events involved in laying out a design is a structured approach to the task. It is only a method chosen to illustrate the thought processes used in laying out a show. There are no hard and fast rules. Do whatever works best for you. The concepts explored are valid for any kind of production, whether a local band gig or major theatrical presentation.

BREAK DOWN THE DESIGN BY EFFECTS

While going through the design scene by scene, the process of breaking the concepts down into effects involves deciding which qualities of light will best deliver the effect you are trying to achieve. As discussed earlier in the book, the qualities of light are intensity, color, form, and movement. Breaking the scenes down into effects may be easier if you first go through each scene, or cue, and list the qualities of light that come into play at that moment. Write down whether the stage should be bright and open, creating energy, or dim and secluded, bringing the levels down. Is there a feeling of mystery or suspense in the scene, or intimacy? This could determine whether the colors lean toward cold or warm. Are you trying to create a calm space or a busy one? This may determine whether the stage is lit with even lighting levels and an even blend of colors or whether the stage has broadly contrasting areas of brightness and darkness and contrasting colors.

While going through the design, note when the audience's attention will be drawn to a particular place. This can be done by keeping the area of interest lit with higher intensities or stronger colors, using the quality of form. Another method of drawing attention to a particular place is to change the lighting on the area at the time the audience is to look there, taking advantage of the quality of movement. Go through the design and note each instance a particular quality of light can be used to obtain the look or action required by the scene.

GROUP THE VARIOUS EFFECTS

Each scene, or lighting cue, must now be described as a grouping or series of lighting effects. A hot stage must be broken down into a golden amber wash, a pale pink beam of light, a background with strong reds and oranges. A murky morning must become blue and lavender lighting with some accent lighting of indigo. At first the listings can be fairly general, as long as you think of your design in terms of actual lighting effects to create the look you want. Go through your design several times. With each pass try to become more specific, envisioning every area of the stage and how you want it to look. Then describe it in terms of the qualities of light. You should still refrain from thinking of the actual lighting fixtures at this point. Think of washes, spots, colors, and intensities of light. Write everything down. It usually helps if you keep things organized. Try creating small charts for each scene, or cue, that allow you to keep track of the colors, intensities (in general terms), and whether an effect is a wash or directed spot.

COMPUTERS IN LIGHTING DESIGN

A computer can be extremely helpful in laying out a design. If everything is laid out in a spreadsheet or

II-iii

a. Opening of scene - Sewer at night
    -murky, feeling of pending danger, quiet, damp, hot, an abundance of shadows,
    visibility poor

b. intro characters
    -building of scene, continue intensity build throughout entrances of characters,
    keep slow and cautious - in line with mood of scene

c. meet begins
    - stage area grows slowly to include full meeting area while keeping the feel
    that the shadows are too dark, hiding too much

d. the coming
    - opposition enters upper level - pull focus - upper level grows in intensity and
    energy level

e. the attack
    -forces join center stage mood heats up as confrontation begins - adds color to
    support heat and tension of scene - lose upper level

f. the death
    -scene collapses on body all else put into silhouette - bring levels down starting
    on outer limits of stage focusing in on body - stage should become similar to top
    of scene - better visibility, highlight on body

g. the police
    -sirens sound pulling some focus up to upper level where a presence is felt - just
    a glow of heat - no flashing lights!!

h. the flight
    -all exits become apparent with slight highlighting as the stage empties of its
    living actors

i. the close
    -whole scene slowly collapses onto body again leaving lasting image in audience's
    eye, as scene goes to black body last to go dark.

A scene breakdown into lighting ideas. Start with broad descriptions to get your ideas down.

SCENE/CUE	INTENSITY	COLOR	FORM	MOVEMENT
II-iii				
a	low levels poor visibility	blues lavenders	high contrast many shadows	
b	low-moderate levels, fair visibility	N/C	N/C	slow build of scene - raise levels
c	moderate levels, fair to good visibility	N/C	N/C	as above
d	N/C	N/C	N/C	build upper level
e	good visibility	add more warmth, reds deep lavenders	N/C	build heat CS
f	lower stage except body which goes up	lose reds	N/C	lose reds and levels focus on body
g	N/C	N/C	N/C	build upper level hint of reds
h	increase exits slightly	N/C	N/C	draw to exits
i	low, poor visibility except body till end	blues	N/C	fade to black draw to body

A breakdown of what each light quality can do for each moment helps create an idea of how the scene should look.

SCENE/CUE	EFFECT DESCRIPTION	CLASS	DIRECTION
II-iii			
a	moon blue wash (L197) - full stage	EFFECT	front SL
	pale blue wash (R63) - area	VISIB	front SR
	pale "warmer" wash (R52?) - area	VISIB	front SL
	indigo wash (L181) - full stage	EFFECT	back SR
	red wash (R24) - full stage	EFFECT	back SL
	purple wash (L126) - full stage	EFFECT	side SR
	rose wash (R47) - full stage	EFFECT	side SL
	blue wash (L120) - full stage	EFFECT	down
b	above plus		
	entrance specials (R54) - tight		various
c	as above		
d	as above		
	upper level special (R48)	EFFECT	side SL
e	as above		
	lavender wash (R58) - main areas	EFFECT	front SR
	warm wash (L109) - full stage	EFFECT	down
f	as above		
	body special (R54) - tight	EFF/VIS	down CS
g	as above		
	upper red special (R27)	EFFECT	up/cyc
h	as above		
i	as above		

The effect breakdown starts becoming more specific as to what is required in each scene.

database program, you will be able to regroup items without constant copying and rewriting. Almost any spreadsheet, database, or integrated program will work. It is often easier to play with the information in a spreadsheet than with most other program types. The integrated packages containing a spreadsheet, database, and word processor in one program can be helpful when preparing documentation of a design, but often each program type is not as thoroughly presented as are stand-alone examples. If an integrated package meets all your needs, however, it can be the best choice. The powerhouse programs many people claim to be the best are often so complicated that understanding them becomes a larger project than the original project you bought the program to solve. There are some excellent programs of all types available at reasonable costs through shareware, just be sure to buy from a reputable supply house. After everything is organized, the information compiled can easily be put into your listings to guide in the execution of your design.

DETERMINE LIGHTING EFFECT CATEGORIES

After the general lighting effects are developed you must break them down further into categories such as general (visibility) lighting, effect lighting, set lighting, etc. This can be made easier by including a column in your charts for entering the category of the item described. After you have broken the scenes down into effects, you can go back and categorize the effects themselves by a simple mark in the column.

Determining what category an effect belongs to can be done in broad strokes. If the effect is one that introduces a general coloring to the entire stage or large stage space, such as an entire acting area, it is a *wash*. If the wash is to be the main lighting for seeing what is taking place on stage at the time it is used, it is *visibility lighting*, often referred to as *area lighting*. If it is only used to help create a mood or look it is an *effect* or *accent wash*. If it is used only to light the setting it is a *set wash*. If the light is more controlled than a wash, lighting a relatively small, specific area, it is a *special*. Again if the special is used to provide the primary light for seeing what is in its focus, it is visibility lighting. If it creates a mood or look, it is *effect lighting*.

HOW TO LIGHT FOR VARIOUS EFFECTS

Once you have determined the general effects and effect categories, you must determine which available methods of lighting would best deliver them. At his point the methods are the directions from which the lighting is coming. This can be accomplished by going through your listing as it stands and evaluating each effect in relation to the rest of the scene or cue. Care must be taken during this stage since this is the point where the final look of the stage is completed. Up to now everything has been moving from very broad to general, though with a little more focus. Now you decide exactly what each effect is to accomplish.

It is very common at this point to add effects to a scene, or to break effects previously listed into two or three effects. The creation of rough sketches at this point can be of further assistance. Visualization of the scene becomes critical. Is the amber wash adding warmth to the scene to be a backlight wash bathing the stage and adding a glow on the actors' heads and shoulders, or a side light wash brushing their cheeks from one side, with a slightly darker tone coming from the other side of the stage but with little color hitting the stage floor? Each scene, or each cue, must be gone over carefully to develop an entire picture, giving the basic color, intensity, and direction of the lighting creating it. The entire composition of the picture must be set up. During this process it is a good idea to start choosing more specific colors for the different effects. As the scene is developed, write down some ideas of gel colors you wish to use, such as Roscolux 59 (R59) or Lee 180 (L180). Having a swatch book of the gels available helps at this stage.

The information gathered up to this point can now be regrouped by lighting position to help determine which effects for different scenes will be able to share instrumentation. You will be able to see repetition of a general front or side wash. Though the exact colors may vary slightly, similar washes will be found several times throughout a design. At this time a color that would work through the show for a grouping of effects can be determined, and these effects can be noted to share a common wash. You will probably find that the effects using washes, for either visibility or accent, can be trimmed down to just a few different ones.

It is less common for specials to be as versatile throughout a design. A special tends to have such a specific purpose that it is impossible to combine one with others. One situation that changes this is when a stage is laid out with a separate dimmer for every lighting fixture. This has great advantages, especially on a smaller stage, because it allows every fixture in a plot to be used as a special. This way each fixture used to make up the general stage lighting can be isolated and used as a special, spotlighting a very specific area. This setup is more costly initially since the cost of dimmers can be high, but it adds an enormous degree of flexibility to a plot, often saving money in fixtures required as well as rehangs required in a house that runs smaller productions along with a larger one. Depending on your fixture inventory and the lighting budget at your disposal, regrouping your listing by position will be helpful later to see where modifications can be made to allow more effects to share instrumentation. It is often advisable to share common effects (when possible) to save hanging space as well as instrumentation. Only a limited number of lighting positions will be available to give the various angles required for a given effect. This is especially true considering that the stage, which is generally small to begin with, will contain a setting of some sort.

ORGANIZING THE STAGE

Before beginning the process of developing the light plot — choosing which fixtures are to be hung and focused where — you must decide how to organize the stage. The most common practice in stage lighting today is to break the setting down into several smaller acting areas and then to light each area with equipment allocated to it. Each effect decided upon in the process described above would be duplicated in each acting area, using separate fixtures for each area. By allowing the areas to overlap you can achieve a very evenly lit stage, avoiding the constant walking in and out of shadows that can be a problem if fixtures lighting adjacent areas are too far apart or coming from angles that are too varied.

To determine how many separate areas are to be lit on stage for the general wash, you may either decide how large each area will be and choose the fixtures that achieve this at a predetermined *throw distance* (the distance a light is from the subject being lit) or calculate how large an area the fixtures you have available cover at that throw distance and arrange your areas accordingly. More acting areas give more control and improve the ability to isolate different areas on the stage. However, the more areas you assign, the more fixtures your plot is going to require. It also becomes more difficult to achieve an even blending of areas as you increase their number. If the flexibility of a large number of smaller areas is not necessary, don't get carried away. To achieve an evenly lit stage you should figure on overlapping each area by 40 to 50% of its diameter. This takes advantage of the normal drop-off at beam edges of most instruments and eliminates shadows when walking from one area to another.

Here is an important point to remember when laying out areas or choosing the fixtures to light them. The most important part of the performer you are lighting is about four to six feet above the stage level — his face. Don't make the common mistake of laying out a floor level plot, providing the stage floor with perfectly even illumination, only to have the performer's face walking in and out of shadows. Unless you are lighting an industrial show for a tennis shoe manufacturer, the real action is a few feet higher up.

BRINGING YOUR DESIGN TO LIFE

Now it is time to determine how your design can be brought to life. Up to this point you have been designing what the lighting is to look like throughout a performance. Now you must determine how to execute the design with the tools at your disposal. The listings you have made to determine the colors, intensities, and directions of the light to create the different effects will prove themselves extremely valuable at this time. By examining your lists of final effects — that is, the washes and specials you have decided are required to create your design — you will be able to determine what fixtures are able to deliver the kind of light you will need for each effect.

Decide whether each effect will require a soft- or hard-edged beam of light, a beam that is a flood or spot of light. Will an effect need precise control over the beam, possibly masking it from nearby items? Try to keep the descriptions as brief as possible, one or two words will most often suffice. Use words such as "soft, hard, flood, spot, shuttered, or sharp" to help determine which lighting fixtures will do the job required. After noting the required characteristics of the actual light beam for each effect, you can pick out effects that require a particular instrument. If an effect must have a hard edge you would generally use an ellipsoidal spotlight. Effects requiring some sort of shuttering need to be further broken down to indicate how precisely they must mask off other areas around them. If a sharp line is required, again, an ellipsoidal will do the job. If a softer edged beam will do, allowing a small blending into adjacent areas, either an ellipsoidal pulled slightly off focus or a fresnel or PAR fixture using barn doors will do. Fixtures that can flood an area include fresnels, PAR's, scoops, floods, even ellipsoidals if one with a wide enough beam angle is chosen. If very large areas are to be covered, either a number of fixtures delivering a soft-edged beam can be blended together, or striplights could be chosen.

One thing to be aware of is that fixtures coming from too many different angles can create so many shadows that the scene can become busy. Also, since the sun only throws one shadow, the effect of sunlight can be destroyed if too many dark or hard shadows are cast all over the stage. If this presents a problem, fewer fixtures from the same angle can be used with various fixtures providing a diffuse beam to fill in. The more diffuse the beam of light projected by the fixture, the softer the shadow will be. The beam of a fixture can be made more diffuse by using one of the diffusion gels available from the makers of plastic color media.

Backgrounds are most often lit using a grouping of striplights, though scoops can also do an excellent job. First you must determine what you need the fixture to do, then choose a fixture that will do it. There are almost always several different fixture types that will carry out a task equally well. Often it becomes a matter of what is available. It is also a good idea to try to use the same instrument type to carry out similar jobs throughout a design when possible. The quality of the light beams of different fixture types can vary enough to be noticeable when an actor walks from area to area

on the stage. Similar effects should also use fixtures lamped with lamps providing similar color temperatures. Though color temperature is not too critical for stage performances, fixtures providing the same intensity beam at different color temperatures will appear quite a bit different. Refer to the section on lamps for more detail on color temperature.

The Choice of a Custom Fixture

There are times no available fixture will allow the creation of the exact effect desired. What do people do in this case? There are two possibilities. The factors involved with deciding which to use involve time and money. Not enough of either eliminates the optimum choice for the designer. The most desirable choice for the designer is to have a custom fixture designed that will do what is needed, if possible. The second choice is to come up with as close a compromise as possible.

The choice of buying a custom fixture is limited to shows with time for development and large budgets. Having a custom stage lighting fixture made for a show first involves contracting a lighting manufacturer to understand the needs of the designer. Next, the manufacturer must conceptualize the actual physical and electrical design of the fixture. After the basic design is approved, a manufacturing production pack must be developed. This is followed by producing and testing a prototype. After the prototype is approved a production run must be scheduled and completed, whether one fixture or six hundred is needed.

This entire project requires both time and money. Though there have been projects that were pushed through the whole process in only a couple of weeks, generally a few months are involved with the development of a custom lighting fixture. The costs of a project of this kind can run into thousands of dollars. Even what seems like a minor change can force a company to go from automated manufacturing methods to hand operations, costing hundreds of dollars more to produce. Most of the custom fixtures designed are for large productions, such as Broadway shows, national tours, and major rock tours. Some of the most interesting projects facing fixture manufacturers involve developing custom fixtures for different shows.

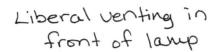
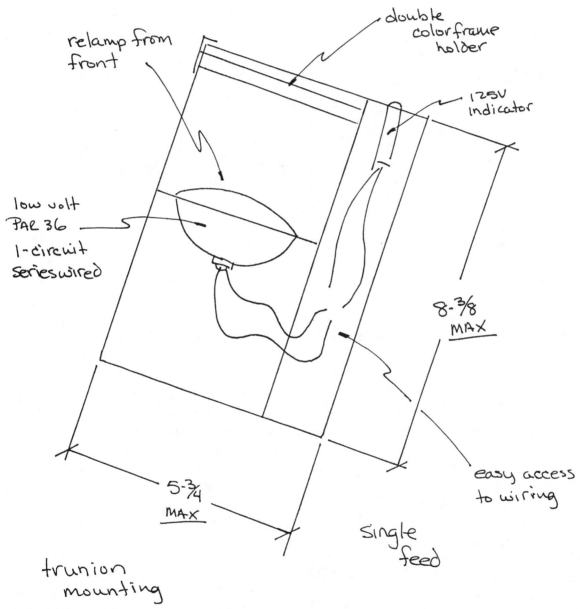

Liberal venting in front of lamp

double colorframe holder

relamp from front

125V indicator

low volt PAR 36 1-circuit serieswired

8-3/8 MAX

easy access to wiring

5-3/4 MAX

single feed

trunion mounting

ALL STEEL WELDED CONSTRUCTION

Initial sketches of a custom fixture are generally rough, with notes about what the limits of the fixture will be.

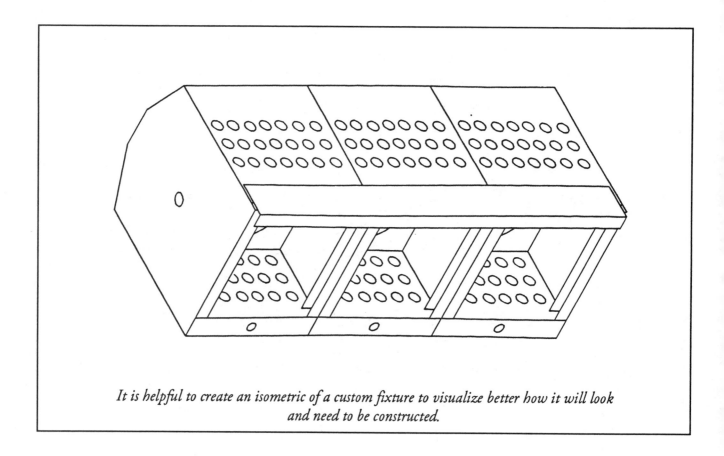

It is helpful to create an isometric of a custom fixture to visualize better how it will look and need to be constructed.

Having the resources of either time or money, let alone both, is fairly uncommon in any but the largest of productions. Most often the designer must come up with a compromise of some kind to solve his dilemma. This can be a very frustrating experience. A common problem is that the more you try to come up with a solution without success, the more important, and critical, the effect seems to become. Don't let your sense of proportion get lost. An entire design has never been ruined for want of a single effect. It is important to remember that most problems are solved by simple solutions. A single beam of light shining through an open window can often convey a bright moonlit night more effectively than an entire bank of projectors armed with specially developed, hand-painted slides.

As a point of interest sometimes a custom lighting fixture project can yield a fixture that proves beneficial to the stage industry as a whole. Such is the case of the mini-strip discussed in the chapter on striplights. This fixture was developed by Lighting & Electronics, Inc., for a production of *La Cage Aux Folles*, the lighting for which was designed by Jules Fisher. The production design required a small striplight delivering a high light output. The engineering staff at Lighting & Electronics worked with the production lighting designer and developed the fixture around the lamp he requested. The end result was the mini-strip, now an industry standard found on almost every major theatrical production and rock tour, with similar fixtures now being produced by several other manufacturers.

THE LIGHT PLOT

After you have determined which instruments you want to use and where you want them to come from, you can start drafting your light plot. For a detailed description of the various pieces of paperwork needed to document a lighting design properly, refer to the chapter on paperwork later in this book. Some designers like to get the physical layout down on paper before working out all the listings, such as the hookup and patch sheet. Other designers prefer to have everything known before starting the plot. You should do what you feel most comfortable doing as long as you work everything out at some point. Do not think your light plot is the final goal of your design. The final goal is to see your design properly executed, and this can only come about if you plan ahead for every detail.

You will have to determine the vertical positioning of the fixtures, also known as the *trim heights*. The people mounting the show need to know where to set the heights of the electrics, or pipes, off which the fixtures hang so that the angles you end up with are the same ones you developed on your design. Sometimes you do not have a choice of heights because the positions available are attached to the walls or ceiling and don't allow for height adjustment. When this is the case you determine the angle at which your lighting fixtures shine down by how close to the lighting position they are focused. If the electrics can be repositioned vertically, you can choose the best height to achieve the focus angle you want. This is easiest to do by drawing an elevation view of the stage with the electrics. As with the other pieces of paperwork, a detailed description of the elevation is given in the chapter on paperwork.

MAINTAINING ORIGINALITY

With experience, many of the stages of laying out a design become automatic, actually becoming an element of the original creation. Looks originate as washes and color choices. Common washes are present at the very beginning of the conceptualization of the design. Favorite fixtures for certain effects are developed and become an immediate response to a needed effect. This can be very advantageous when time is restricted; however, care must be taken that you do not become stale and automatic. Some people develop a set of looks and washes that they rotate through every show they design. Breaking away from them becomes increasingly more difficult if the effort isn't made to create fresh ideas for different shows all the time. Having some solutions or tools to solve general problems is effective as long as you use them creatively, generating new designs for each production.

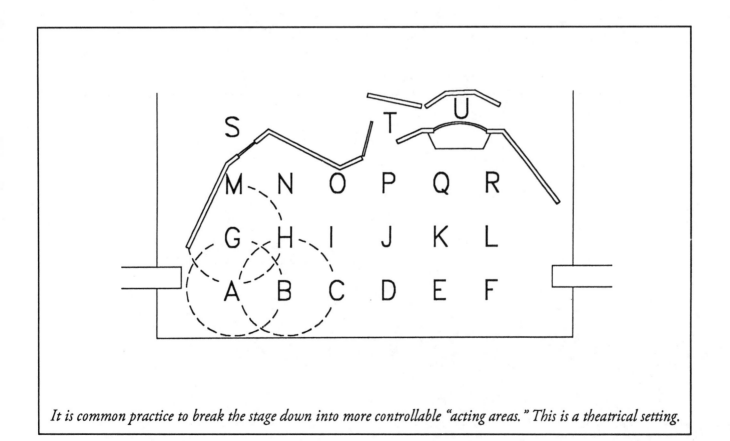

It is common practice to break the stage down into more controllable "acting areas." This is a theatrical setting.

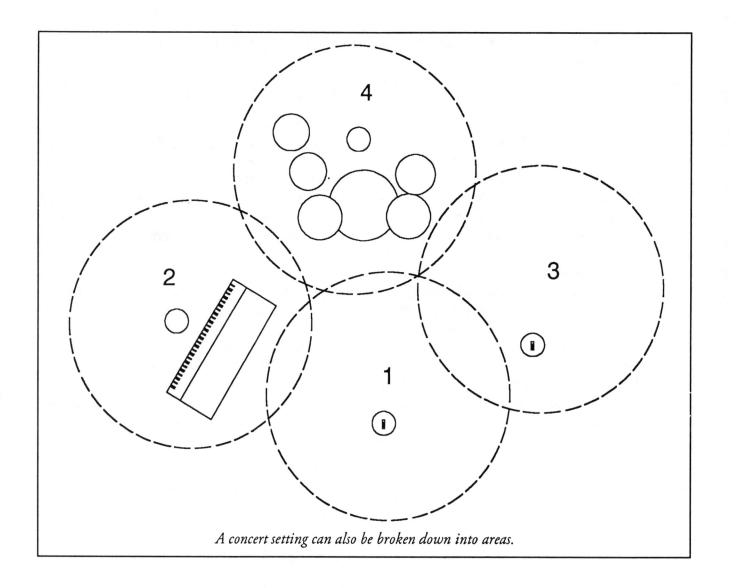

A concert setting can also be broken down into areas.

PART II
Equipment

Introduction to Equipment

Today's market offers a wide variety of different lighting instrument types to choose from when planning your lighting design. The most commonly used are PAR's, ellipsoidals, fresnels, scoops, and striplights (or borders). The following pages detail information about the more common fixture types and applications. Although the information is similar within each instrument type, you will find some design differences among various fixture manufacturers. Some specific lamp information is not included due to the large number of lamps used; photometric information regarding specific lamps should be available through your fixture supplier. See Appendix 2 for some general photometric information on several of the more common fixture/lamp combinations. Appendix 5 shows the wiring layouts for the four most commonly used connectors installed on stage lighting fixtures.

GENERAL SAFETY

Whenever you are dealing with stage lighting equipment, your primary concern should be *safety*, yours and everyone else's. Several hazards can be associated with stage lighting — things falling (causing personal injury); things burning (burn and fire hazards); things frying (electrical shock hazards). By "things" I mean items *and* people.

When equipment is improperly secured, positioned, handled, or maintained, any of the above hazards can become reality. A reality that can end in property loss, severe injury and death. You can reduce the chance of these hazards occurring. Some tips on keeping things safe are:

- Don't assume things are hung safely. Always check. Falling hazards can be prevented by having second-

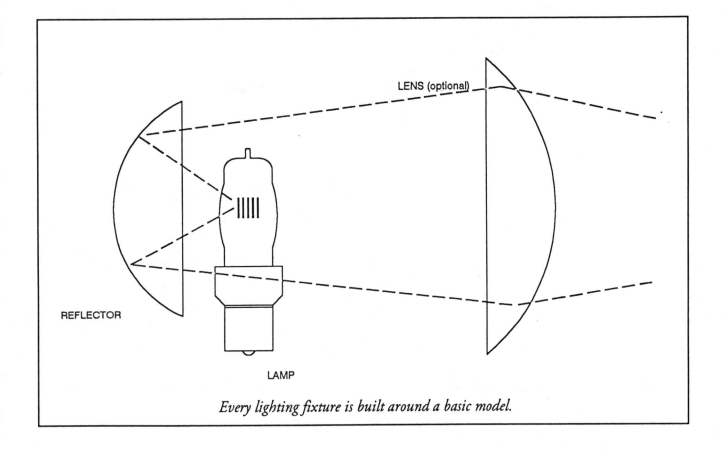

LENS (optional)

REFLECTOR

LAMP

Every lighting fixture is built around a basic model.

ary safeties keeping equipment in place. Check fasteners for tightness once in a while when lighting fixtures are hanging for some time.

- Burns and fires can be prevented by making sure hot instruments are kept safely away from people's body parts and other materials (such as wood or drapery) that can be burned or ignited by them. Don't touch a lighting fixture without making sure it isn't too hot to touch. Insulating gloves are commonly used to prevent burns. Almost any stage lighting fixture gets hot enough to cause burns and fires.

- Everyone knows how dangerous electricity can be. A worn piece of insulation or broken wire can expose people to potentially lethal shock hazards. Don't touch anything without making sure it's not energized. Unplug fixtures before opening them or putting your hand in them for any reason. Always know what you're about to touch. Make a habit of regularly inspecting your equipment and repair anything that begins to show signs of wear. Frayed

insulation and wires or loose electrical connections can be dangerous to you and everyone around you.

Don't underestimate how dangerous it can be when you misuse or abuse your lighting equipment.

Earlier I described what designers do when they need a custom lighting fixture. You should note that experienced fixture designers are always involved. Homemade lighting fixtures can be extremely dangerous. In order to produce the brightness of light needed in the theater, light sources that generate incredible amounts of heat are used. Temperatures can be reached that will quickly break down the insulation of ordinary wiring or melt through most common materials used for building sets and, unfortunately, homemade lights. Be careful.

BEAM SPREAD FACTOR

You will find included in the information on some of the units something called the *beam spread factor*. This number is the product of a formula involving the

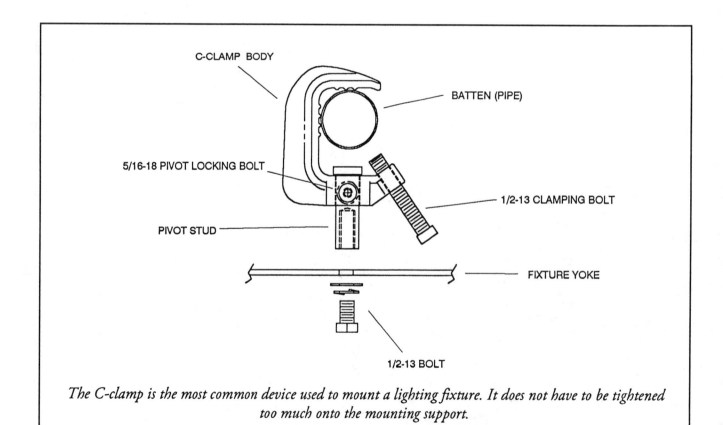

The C-clamp is the most common device used to mount a lighting fixture. It does not have to be tightened too much onto the mounting support.

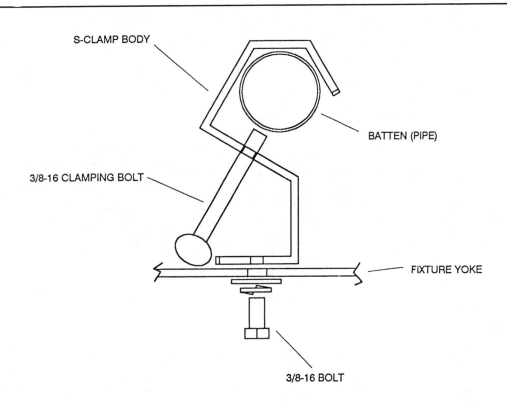

S-CLAMP BODY

BATTEN (PIPE)

3/8-16 CLAMPING BOLT

FIXTURE YOKE

3/8-16 BOLT

The S-clamp is most commonly associated with smaller PAR's in music and club applications.

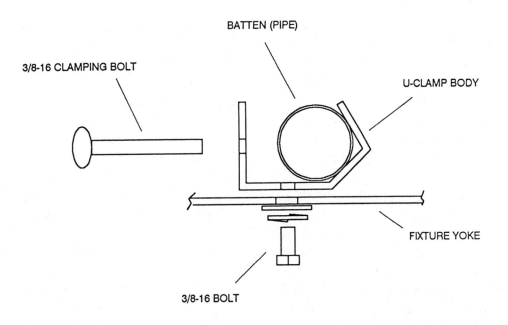

3/8-16 CLAMPING BOLT

BATTEN (PIPE)

U-CLAMP BODY

FIXTURE YOKE

3/8-16 BOLT

The U-clamp was developed to allow mounting units on pipes flush to a club ceiling.

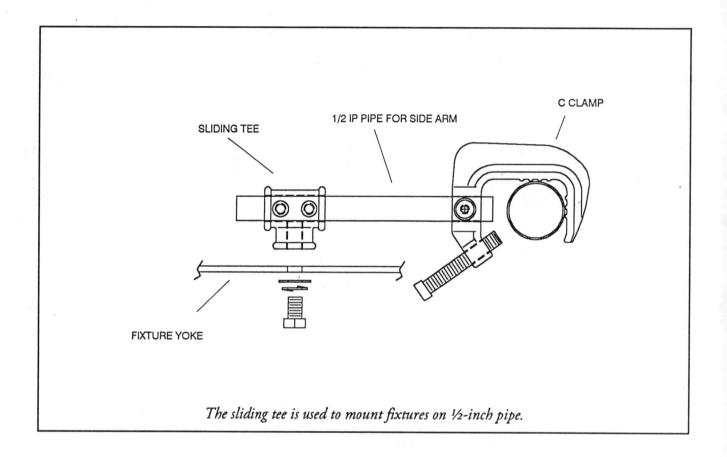

SLIDING TEE

1/2 IP PIPE FOR SIDE ARM

C CLAMP

FIXTURE YOKE

The sliding tee is used to mount fixtures on ½-inch pipe.

beam or field angles of a fixture. It is used to determine how large an area an instrument can cover at a given throw distance. The actual formula used to derive the beam spread factor is:

beam spread factor = 2 x tangent(beam angle/2)

Every instrument has a *beam angle* (the angle at which you have 50% of full intensity at the edges of the beam) and a *field angle* (the angle at which you have 10% of full intensity at the edges of the beam). Every angle has a beam spread factor that can be derived from it. Appendix 3 gives spread factors for different beam angles. To use the beam spread factor of an angle, you just multiply the *throw distance* (distance from lighting instrument to subject being lit) by the beam spread factor. The result is the diameter of the beam at the given throw distance in whatever unit of measure was used for the throw distance. The reason a beam spread factor is not given for all the lighting instruments covered in the text is that in some instruments beam angles are determined by the lamp used as opposed to the fixture itself. Many of these are covered in the Appendix.

PURCHASING FOR QUALITY AND VALUE

When purchasing stage lighting instruments, be certain to look carefully at each unit. Ask yourself if it is the best value you can find. Sometimes a less expensive instrument is worth less but not always. Compare units supplied by different manufacturers. Look at the hardware used on the fixture. Are the materials used of adequate quality? What is the highest wattage lamp it is rated to use? Make sure the metal used is of heavy enough gauge (thickness) to hold up to your needs. Look at the finish, is it covered well enough? Does the unit look as though it will endure many load-ins and load-outs? Take your time when shopping for lighting instruments and compare those made by different manufacturers. An inexpensive unit can more than double its cost if it doesn't hold up. You should also ask to see a unit in use and compare its output to what is on the specification sheets. Many manufacturers' spec sheets are a bit optimistic about their products' performance. Be sure the equipment you are going to buy gives you what you need. Do not rely solely on spec sheets.

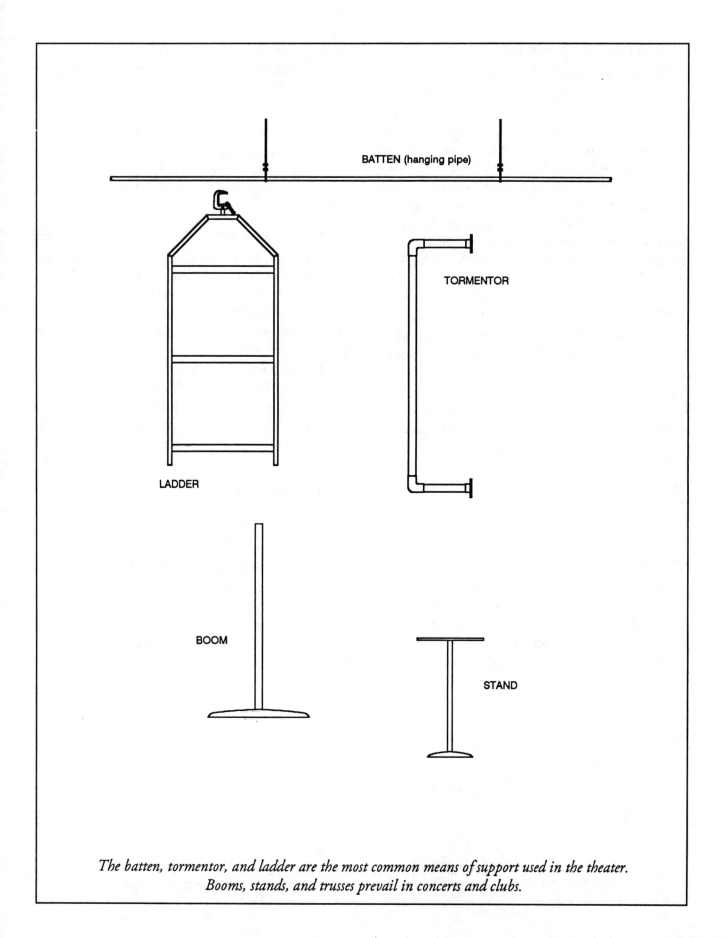

The batten, tormentor, and ladder are the most common means of support used in the theater.
Booms, stands, and trusses prevail in concerts and clubs.

MOUNTING INSTRUMENTS

C-Clamps, S-Clamps, U-Clamps

Lighting instruments can be mounted in several ways. The most common is the stage C-clamp. The clamp is attached to the fixture yoke using a 1/2-13 hex bolt. It is then placed onto a light batten (pipe) and the 1/2-13 square head bolt on the clamp is tightened onto the batten. This bolt need only be snugged against the batten enough to stop the clamp from slipping. It is common for people to overtighten these bolts, causing eventual failure in the hardware or clamp. Variations of the C-clamp are the S-clamp and the U-clamp. Both work in basically the same manner, often employing ⅜-inch hardware instead of the ½-inch found on the C-clamp. S- and U-clamps are less expensive and are used for lighter fixtures such as PAR's and small fresnels. The U-clamp is slightly different in that it hangs under the batten from which the fixture hangs. This saves some space and allows hanging off a batten or pipe that is flush to the wall or ceiling. Care must be taken, however, to provide some form of safety to catch the fixture should the clamp loosen. This is more important with the U-clamp than any other type of clamp since it is the only one that does not have part of the clamp overhanging the batten to which it is attached. This means if its bolt should loosen slightly, the fixture will fall.

Sliding Tee

Another device used to mount fixtures is the *sliding tee*. The tee is most often used with a *sidearm*. After mounting the tee to the fixture in the same manner as the C-clamp, it slides onto a piece of ½-inch pipe, which is supported on one end (a sidearm is supported by a C-clamp on one end). Using this arrangement allows a fixture to be mounted in its proper hanging position off a vertical pipe.

Fixtures may be hung off pipes hanging from the ceiling (battens), pipes mounted on a wall (tormentors), sidearms attached to pipe mounted vertically in a base (booms), a variety of lighting stands, and aluminum trussing (available in a large variety of shapes and sizes).

"Safetying" Fixtures

Whenever a fixture is hung it should be "safetied" off to the batten or pipe from which it is hanging. This is most often done with a safety cable — a length of wire rope with a loop in one end and a spring clip on the other. The safety cable is looped over the pipe and then either attached directly to the fixture or looped through its yoke. This practice is too often neglected. A fixture falling from its position can seriously injure or kill someone. Don't forget this practice. If you do not have safety cables, rope will do, just don't attach it to an area on the fixture that will get too hot and create a potential fire hazard.

WORDS TO REMEMBER

When working with stage lighting instruments always remember:

Stage lights get very hot.

A lighting fixture should never be touched with bare hands after it has been on for a couple of moments. Temperatures exceeding 500° F are not uncommon on the outside surfaces of lighting instruments. The inside of the instrument gets even hotter.

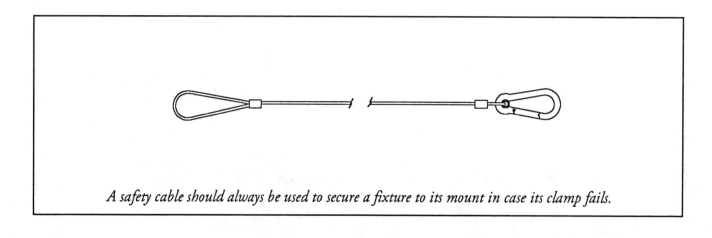

A safety cable should always be used to secure a fixture to its mount in case its clamp fails.

ENTERTAINMENT LIGHTING COMPANY

Box 1123 · 34 Spring Road
Sampson, WY 55555-5555
1-800-555-1111

ELLIPSOIDAL SPOTLIGHT

CAT.NO. ESP12

SPECIFICATIONS:

The luminaire shall be a UL approved 500 to 750 watt ellipsoidal with a medium two pin socket, to accept an axially mounted tungsten halogen lamp, housed inside a double flatted Alzak aluminum reflector. The fixture shall be constructed of an all welded steel body with cast aluminum lamp housing and cap. The unit shall have four stainless steel shutters and a template slot mounted within the body. The two 6 x 12 lenses shall be of heat resistant borosilicate mounted in an adjustable steel lens tube complete with locking thumb screw for beam definition. The lens holder shall be equipped with steel color frame holders on the sides and bottom. A hinged body, via locking thumb screw, allows access to the interior of the reflector housing and shutter assembly. Ventilating ports shall be baffled for cooler operation with minimal light leakage.

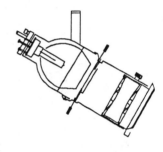

Relamping shall be accomplished from the rear of the unit, without disturbing the prefocused alignment, by unthreading the brass thumb screw and removing the adjustable lamp and socket assembly from the unit.

Lamp focusing shall be accomplished by adjusting the four focusing screws on the axial cap.

The luminaire shall be supplied with an iron C clamp suitable for use on up to 2" OD pipe, rigid strap yoke, color frame, safety cable, and a three foot three wire lead in a black fiberglass sleeve. The exterior of the unit shall be baked charcoal hammertone enamel, the interior lens tube finish shall be matte black enamel.

Entertainment Lighting prides itself on being able to give our customers what they want how they want it and when they want it.

For special applications please call and inquire about our custom capabilties

---

Data sheets are available from manufacturers to give the specifics about each of their lighting fixtures.

ELLIPSOIDAL SPOTLIGHT

CAT.NO. ESP12

DIMENSIONS: 7-5/8"x7-5/8"x19-1/2"
WEIGHT: 18 lb

ACCESSORIES:

C-CLAMP
COLOR FRAME
IRIS
PATTERN HOLDER

LAMPS & ILLUMINATION:

EHD 500W 3000°K 2000hr .68 mf   **EHG** 750W 3000°K 2000hr 1.00 mf
EHC 500W 3200°K 300hr   .82 mf   **EHF** 750W 3200°K 300hr   1.32 mf

To find illumination for alternate lamp multiply footcandles by mf (lamp multiplying factor) ie, 128 x .68 = 87 fc with EHD
To find beam diameter at any distance multiply distance x amf (angle multiplying factor) ie, 24 x 0.46 = 11' diameter at 24 feet
To find output in footcandles at any distance : CBCP / (throw distance)^2 = fc   ie 115,000/(24 x 24) = 199.6 fc

All information below based on unit with EHG lamp.

Distance (in feet)	15	30	45	60	75	90
Footcandles	511	128	57	32	20	14

CBCP (center beam candlepower): 115,000

Field angle (10% of CBCP) : 26°   (0.46 amf)

Beam angle (50% of CBCP): 11°   (0.19 amf)

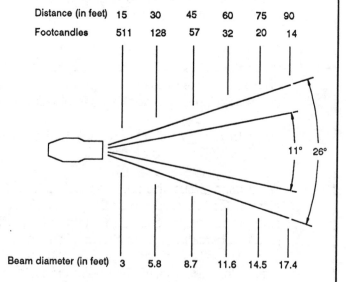

11°   26°

Beam diameter (in feet)	3	5.8	8.7	11.6	14.5	17.4

Complete photometric information is usually found on the data sheet.

Lamps

One category of equipment that is rarely studied and often taken for granted when dealing with stage lighting is lamps. Making the wrong choice when deciding which lamp to use in a fixture can result in less than satisfactory performance. It can even bring about premature lamp or fixture failure if the limits specified for either the lamp or fixture are exceeded. A small point of semantics is that a device used to project the light beam is called an *instrument, fixture,* or *light,* not a lamp. The device put into the fixture to produce the light is called a *lamp,* not a bulb. The bulb is only the clear casing containing the gas and filament arrangement found in a lamp.

LAMP DESIGNS

There are several lamp designs commonly used in stage lighting fixtures. The different lamp types are categorized by both their bulb shape and base type. Most lamps used in stage lighting are listed in the stage/studio catalogs of the various lamp manufacturers. The bulb shapes are usually designated by an initial or initials. The most common shapes used are "A" for Arbitrary, "PS" for Pear-shaped, "T" for Tubular, "G" for Globular, "R" for Reflector, and "PAR" for Parabolic Aluminized Reflector.

The socket/lamp base types most often used in the manufacture of stage/studio lamps are the medium prefocus, mogul prefocus, medium two-pin, prefocus two-pin, medium screw, minican, medium prong, mogul prong, double contact bayonet, and recessed single contact. The medium bi-pin and mogul bi-pin designs are still in use for television and film fixtures, but are not often found in theatrical fixtures any longer. Most often the lamps with the smallest, or most compact, filaments will be found in the focusing instruments, such as the ellipsoidal spotlights, fresnels, etc. These would most often be either tubular or globular shaped lamps. This allows the fixture to work with as near a true point of light as possible.

Fixtures intended to flood the light as much as possible will most often have lamps with larger filaments or integral reflectors and lenses. Fixtures such as striplights, scoops, and floods fit into this category. Lamps used by these fixtures would include A lamps, PS lamps, and the double-ended tubular lamps. Many of these fixtures also utilize the R and PAR lamps. These lamps are a little different in that they are actually a small lighting fixture themselves, incorporating a compact filament design within a reflector and lens arrangement.

LAMP CODES

A system of codes identifying lamps has been created, called the ANSI codes. Each code is a three-letter designation representing a specific lamp. (Example: A 750W, 3,000°K, tungsten halogen lamp with a medium two-pin base is known as an EHG.) Lamps are also known by another coding system, now used mostly for incandescent lamps. You might recognize some of them as 750W T12, 500W T20, 1000W G40, 300W PAR 56, etc. The numbers appearing

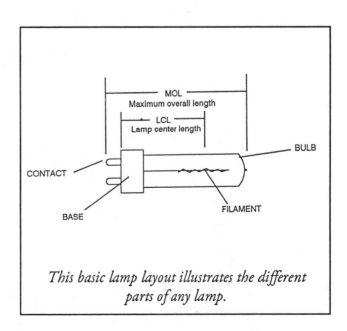

This basic lamp layout illustrates the different parts of any lamp.

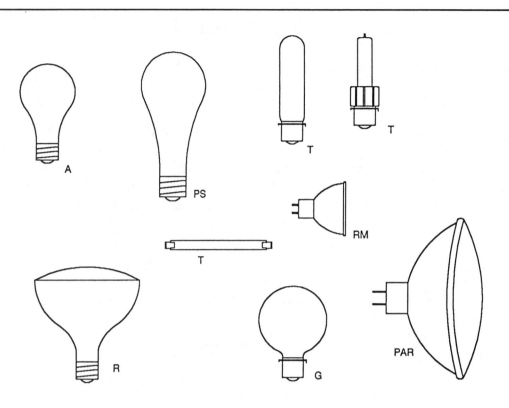

The lamp bulb shapes are given a letter to indicate the class of the lamp's bulb.

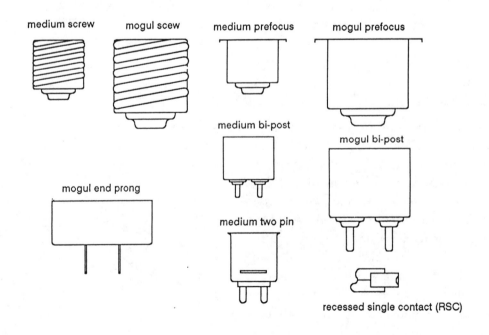

All lamp base types have a code to indicate the socket required.

before the "W" indicate the wattage, the "W" standing for wattage. The letter following the "W" is the bulb shape, "T" meaning Tubular, "G" meaning Globular, and PAR meaning Parabolic Aluminized Reflector. The number following the bulb shape is the diameter of the bulb in eighths of an inch.

CHOOSING LAMPS

Generally, every lighting instrument has a variety of lamps that can be used in it. Within the different lamp groups differences among the lamps relate to hour life, candlepower, color temperature, and wattage. Most lamp manufacturers have specification booklets available for their lamps.

Hour life should be taken into consideration when choosing a lamp. A lamp whose initial cost is one-half that of another lamp, but whose hour life is one-tenth of that other lamp, is not a bargain unless it is superior in some other aspect. You should also be aware of the lamp's recommended burning position. Burning a lamp in a position outside its suggested range will greatly reduce its hour life. You should take care not to touch the clear bulb of a lamp, whether it is quartz or incandescent. The heat burns the oil left by your skin, shortening the life of the lamp.

MEASURING BRIGHTNESS AND OTHER FACTORS

Another factor usually shown for a lamp or a lamp and fixture combination is *candlepower*. All you actually have to understand about candlepower is that it is a measure of quantity, and the higher the candlepower, the brighter the light. Candlepower is measured in *candela*. The unit of measure generally used to represent the brightness of the light at a given place is the *footcandle*. A movie theater is about 5 footcandles, a brightly lit room is between 30 and 50 footcandles, the set of a news broadcast is usually about 150 footcandles, and a brightly lit stage is between 150 and 300 footcandles. To convert the candlepower of a lamp (or lighting fixture) to footcandles, you simply divide the candlepower by the square of the distance in feet the subject is from the light source. (Example: 11,500 candlepower at 10 feet = 11,500 divided by 10 x 10 = 115 footcandles).

$$\text{footcandles} = \text{candlepower}/(\text{throw distance})2$$

This equation only works if the distance is at least ten times the largest dimension of the lighting fixture opening. For instance, this equation can only be used with a PAR 64 (8-inch diameter) for distances greater than approximately 6½ feet (80 inches). At any point on the stage all instruments focused on the same object would, in the same sightline, add together. For example, back light would not add to the illumination level produced by the front lighting on the front of an object. It would, however, add to the level on the floor or possibly the top of an object. You should note that a lamp's brightness changes approximately 3.5% for every 1% its supply voltage changes. This means if a lamp delivering 13,000 candlepower at 120 volts were to be dimmed to receive only 119 volts (120 volts less 1%) it would only deliver approximately 12,545 candlepower (13,000 less 3.5%).

Effects of Color Media

To determine the light output of a lamp or fixture colored using commercially available plastic color media, or gel, multiply the normal output without color by the "Y" factor or "% transmission" rating of the gel. If a lamp/fixture combination usually delivers 100 footcandles without color and you are going to gel it using Lee Filters #101 (Y = 80%), the gelled output would be approximately 80 footcandles (100 x .80 = 80).

$$\text{gelled footcandles} = \text{white footcandles} \times Y \text{ factor}$$

This information is usually given for each color in a color manufacturer's swatch book. The result of using this formula is only approximate and will generally be slightly less than what would be found using a light meter to measure the actual output. Some of the difference is due to the color balancing of the meter, and it is most pronounced with blues and greens.

In film or video lighting, color temperature is an important factor. Color temperatures are given in degrees Kelvin and are used to indicate the degree of whiteness in light. Black is considered 0° Kelvin (K). Most film and video lighting requires light of 3200°K. Sunlight is approximately 5500°K; a clear blue sky between 12,000 and 20,000°K; a candle's flame 1900°K . Because of the required lamp architecture, it is common for lamps with a high color temperature to have shorter lives than similar lamps with lower color temperatures. Also, as a lamp is dimmed its color temperature decreases, moving toward yellow. Increasing the voltage increases the color temperature, going more toward blue or white. The actual amount of change depends on the particular lamp; however, it is safe to say an approximate shift of 125°K occurs for each 10% of voltage change. When choosing a fixture or lamp, try not to use one that is too powerful for the application. A 1000W lamp constantly dimmed down to give you 100 footcandles on stage will often look less intense than a 500W lamp at full intensity (also delivering 100 footcandles). Higher color temperatures appear whiter and therefore brighter.

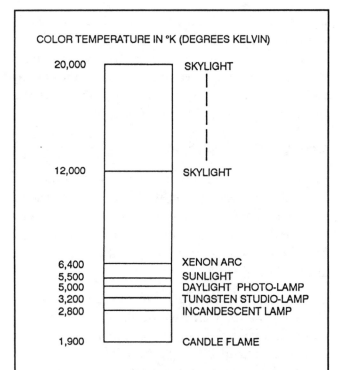

The color temperature chart shows where different lamps and light sources fall in relation to each other.

PAR Lights

A PAR light is basically a "can" designed to make the use of the PAR lamp practical. It is the workhorse instrument in concert lighting and is fighting for the same recognition in theater applications. PAR's are versatile, durable, and lightweight instruments to be used when a focusing instrument (one having a controllable beam) is not actually needed. PAR lamps are available in beam spreads that range from very narrow (10° field angle or .18 beam spread factor) to very wide (135° field angle or 4.83 beam spread factor). Actually, the shape of the beam from a PAR light is often oblong, so the beams have two dimensions, width and length. For example, a 1000W PAR 64 NSP (narrow spot) has a beam factor of .25 by .55. The direction this oblong goes is controlled by actually reaching into the back of the instrument and turning the socket and lamp.

PAR lights are very simple to use. There is really nothing to do other than lamping and focusing (aiming). On the PAR 64, 56, and 46 instruments, relamping is achieved by opening the back of the instrument, squeezing together and removing a spring ring if the instrument utilizes one (unplug the socket first by pulling it straight off, so it doesn't get in the way when removing the ring), and replacing the lamp. A PAR 38 instrument relamps by unscrewing the lamp from the front. Depending on the lamp chosen, a PAR light can be used for everything from specials to general washes.

SPECIFICATIONS

The following is a listing of some of the specifications of most of the PAR light fixtures.

PAR 64

Mogul end prong socket — burn any direction
10 x 10 colorframe
Any 120V PAR 64 lamp with mogul end prong base
Diameter of instrument 10½", length 17", weight with lamp 9½ lbs.
Also available in aluminum to save weight (approx. 3 lbs. less)

PAR 56

Mogul end prong socket — burn any direction
7½ x 7½ colorframe
Any 120V PAR 56 lamp with mogul end prong base
Diameter of instrument 7½", length 14½", weight with lamp 7 lbs.
Also available in aluminum to save weight (approx. 2½ lbs. less)

PAR 46

Medium side prong socket — burn any direction
6 x 6 colorframe
Any 120V PAR 46 lamp with medium side prong base
Diameter of instrument 6½", length 12", weight with lamp 5 lbs.

PAR 38

Medium screw socket
7½ x 7½ colorframe
Any 120V PAR 38 or R40 lamp with medium screw base
Diameter of instrument 7¾", length 9", weight with lamp 4½ lbs.

NARROW BEAM PAR LIGHT EFFECTS

The PAR line is completed by several items used for a specific effect: very narrow, intense shafts of light. These instruments can be used to produce tight spots, or the actual shaft of light can be made visible if the air has smoke or fog in it. There are PAR reflector conversion kits, rainlights (or pinspots), and ACL lights (ACL stands for aircraft landing). Both the rainlights and the ACL lights are low voltage lamps. To allow them to be used with 120 volt feed, they must incorporate a transformer or be wired in series (a specific electrical configuration). No transformer should be dimmed unless the dimmer and transformer are compatible (using a dimmer rated for inductive loads); otherwise, they tend to burn themselves up. If

PAR "cans." Courtesy Lighting & Electronics.

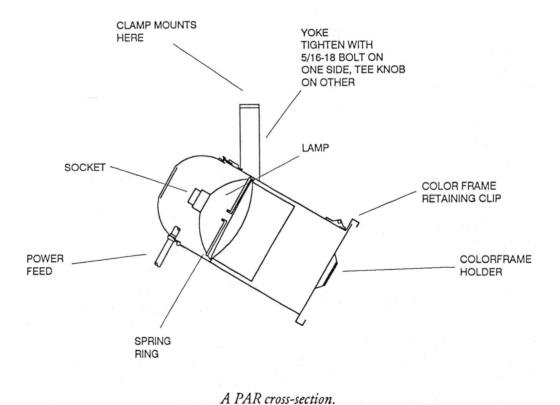

A PAR cross-section.

the lights are wired together in series with a number of instruments whose lamp voltages total approximately 120 volts without transformers, they can be dimmed.

PAR REFLECTOR CONVERSION KITS

These kits consist of a reflector, a socket, and often an adapter lead that fits into either a PAR 64 or a PAR 56 unit. They are also known as ray kits, ray lights, and just kits. Once the conversion is completed, the unit uses a 600W, 3200°K, 120 volt DYS lamp. The beam that it produces is very close to that of a 1000W PAR 64 VNSP (very narrow spot), delivering approximately 300,000 candlepower. The 600W figure is very practical if you use dimmers whose capacities are multiples of 600.

The conversion kit reflector mounts in the fixture the same way as a regular PAR lamp. Then you plug in the new socket with the adapter leads. After the conversion, relamping can be done through the front of the instrument if there is no safety screen present. Care should be taken when handling the leads. It is not uncommon for the leads to be broken off the socket, rendering the reflector kit useless. The unit should also be checked periodically to make sure the adapters do not fall out of the fixture socket. It is no great problem if both fall out, but if only one does, a dead short can be created.

You should be aware that not all reflector kits are the same. The better kits are made with actual specular clear anodized aluminum reflectors (Alzak is a trade name, owned by Alcoa, for this process). Plated reflectors not only tend to blister and peel in time; the plating also absorbs as much as 10% of the light, though it appears visually more reflective. Reflectors made of raw aluminum oxidize when exposed to the heat put out by the lamp.

RAINLIGHTS

Rainlights, or pinspots, are extremely popular in clubs. They are used to spot mirrorballs or as down spots on dance floors. They are very bright, with extremely narrow beams. They are available for use with either PAR 36 or PAR 46 6.4 volt lamps. The lamps are changed on both instruments by removing a spring ring from the front of the instrument, taking out the lamp, unscrewing the leads from the back of the lamp, and then reversing the process.

PAR 36 Rainlight (Pin Spot)

6 x 6 colorframe

GE 4515 30W 6.4V lamp (actually any PAR 36 lamp 6.4V 30W or less)

Diameter of instrument 6", length 8½", weight with lamp 5 lbs.

PAR 46 Rainlight (Pin Spot)

7½ x 7½ colorframe

GE 4535 30W 6.4V lamp (actually any PAR 46 lamp 6.4V 30W or less)

Diameter of instrument 7½", length 8½", weight with lamp 5 lbs.

ACL LIGHTS

ACL lights use 28 volt lamps that are extremely bright, with extremely narrow beam spreads. The lamps are used in standard PAR fixtures. They generally produce between 100,000 and 600,000 candlepower and have beam spread factors of between .19 and .26. One disadvantage of these lamps is that they have very short hour lives — 10 to 25 hours. The lamps are replaced the same way as standard PAR lamps with screw terminals.

ACL STRIPS

ACL strips are units made up of four PAR instruments wired in series. Since their total voltages are approximately 120V, they are dimmable. There are PAR 36 and 46 ACL strips available. The PAR 36 fixtures are smaller and less intense than the PAR 46 fixtures. When choosing an ACL strip, some features to look for are how far the lamp is set back in each individual "can" (the farther back they are set, the better the separation between beams) and whether it is possible to gel each "can" to produce four different colored shafts of light.

Ellipsoidal Spotlights

The ellipsoidal spotlight belongs to a group of instruments referred to as *focusing instruments*. The ellipsoidal has been the prominent instrument used in theatrical stage lighting. With the ellipsoidal you can vary the edge of the beam from a sharp to a soft focus, and you can cut in the beam to keep the light off places you wish to remain unlit by a particular instrument. Because of the large amount of control you have over the beam this instrument creates, it is generally used wherever precision is required. Ellipsoidals are commonly seen being used for specials, front of house lighting (where you may want to cut in the beam off the proscenium walls), side lighting (when a specific path is required), and pattern projecting. When determining the beam diameter projected by an ellipsoidal in sharp focus, you should use its field angle information.

There is a large variety of ellipsoidals, ranging from a mini-ellipsoidal for short throws to a 6 x 22 for long throws. They are generally designated by the lens type used, such as 6 x 9, 6 x 12, 4H x 6H, etc. The first number refers to the front lens diameter in inches; the second to the focal length of the lens. The *focal length* of a lens is the distance from some point in the lens (assume the center for convenience) to the point where all light rays coming from a distant light source and passing through the lens are concentrated by the lens. The point of concentration is known as the *focal point* of the lens. If you are ever faced with having to determine the approximate focal length of a plano-convex (PC) lens, take it to where direct sunlight can pass through it since the sun is the best "distant" source of light. Use the lens to focus the sunlight into a small point of light on a smooth surface. The

Axial ellipsoidal spotlights. Courtesy Lighting & Electronics.

distance from the center of the lens to the surface you are projecting onto is the approximate focal length of the lens. There are also some zoom ellipsoidals that combine the beam spreads of several of the fixed focal length instruments. These instruments are often called out by their field angles in degrees, as are many of the newer 1000W fixtures. In a standard fixed focal length ellipsoidal, the longer the focal length, the narrower the beam angle or spread.

TYPES OF ELLIPSOIDALS

There are two major groups of ellipsoidal spotlights: the *axial quartz* and the *incandescent.* As you probably guess, these names refer to the type of lamp used in the instrument. The quartz lamp is fast becoming the standard since it does not darken with age (as incandescent lamps do), often has a longer hour life, and is becoming more readily available than incandescent lamps. The incandescent ellipsoidal uses a T12 lamp, such as the 500W DNS or 750W DNT. The axial quartz ellipsoidal uses a medium two-pin, quartz halogen lamp such as the 500W EHD or the 750W EHG. All fixtures have a maximum wattage rating that should be recognized. Exceeding it will increase light output but will also result in some fixture breakdown, such as burnt shutters, cracked lenses, and possibly electrical wiring failure.

FOCUSING

The ellipsoidal spotlight is a little more trouble to focus than are most stage lighting instruments. This is because of the amount of control you have over the beam it produces. To harden or soften the edge of the beam, you slide the lens holder at the front of the instrument either forward or back, *after* loosening the screw located behind the color frame holder on the top or bottom of the unit. If you wish to cut in the edge of the beam, you slide in one or more of the four shutters located at approximately the center of the instrument. Since the lenses invert the beam, the shutter opposite the edge you wish to cut in is used (left for right, top for bottom ...).

If the instrument is equipped with an *iris,* the iris handle is usually located just in front of one of the shutters and is used to control the diameter of the beam. If you use the instrument to project a pattern, you can either slip the pattern into a pattern holder and then into the slot located in front of the top shutter, or on some you can open the barrel by loosening the thumb screw located just in front of the slot, place the pattern inside the instrument, and close the instrument. Use of a pattern holder is the most convenient. If you are going to use an ellipsoidal for a smaller diameter beam than it normally produces for prolonged periods, it is not a good idea to use an iris. It will burn out in short time. Using a piece of sheet metal of fairly heavy gauge with the correct diameter punched in it works better. Pie tins with different size holes can be used to determine the size required for your application. With most 6-inch units available, an approximate hole diameter in inches may be determined by dividing the beam diameter you want by the beam diameter the fixture would normally give at your throw distance (use the field angle information to determine this). Then multiply the answer by three, which is the diameter generally found in the center of a 6-inch ellipsoidal. Some companies that supply patterns have diameter sets that will probably last longer than an iris but not as long as heavier gauge steel or aluminum.

RELAMPING

Relamping is achieved by opening a cap or door at the back of the instrument, generally by unscrewing a knurled screw, and with an incandescent instrument pushing the lamp slightly in, turning it counterclockwise, and pulling it out. With an axial quartz instrument, you simply pull the lamp straight out. You then reverse either procedure to complete relamping. You should never touch the clear bulb of a lamp, whether quartz or incandescent, with your skin. The oils from your skin shorten the life of the lamp drastically.

TROUBLESHOOTING

Since the lamp and the reflector are separate parts of the instrument, all ellipsoidals need periodic realignment to make sure the filament of the lamp is at or near the focal point of the reflector. If the lamp is not aligned properly in the reflector, you will not get the optimum light output. Alignment is carried out while focusing the instrument on a flat, matte surface (white is generally preferred) about ten feet away. Adjust the barrel so that you have the hardest edge you can achieve. (If the instrument is badly out of alignment you may have to keep adjusting this throughout the process.) On many instruments you then adjust the three screws on the cap of the instrument until you have the brightest, most even field. The screw in the center of the three adjustment screws is used to lock the position of the socket plate; you must loosen it to proceed.

Some ellipsoidals have a joystick setup for alignment. Lamp position is adjusted by loosening and moving the joystick located at the back of the fixture to achieve the best field. This feature is convenient when aligning the unit but tends to invite the unwary to move it around when not required and often puts the fixture out of alignment. On instruments that incorporate a joystick setup, the lamp depth adjustment is normally separate. The optimum design has the depth adjustment independent of the lamp access for relamping. This is not the case with most joystick-type fixtures,

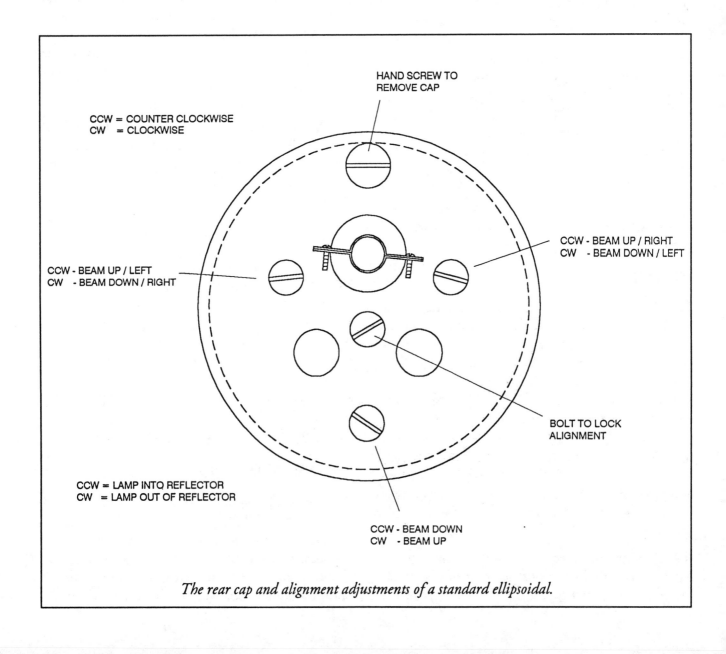

HAND SCREW TO
REMOVE CAP

CCW = COUNTER CLOCKWISE
CW   = CLOCKWISE

CCW - BEAM UP / RIGHT
CW   - BEAM DOWN / LEFT

CCW - BEAM UP / LEFT
CW   - BEAM DOWN / RIGHT

BOLT TO LOCK
ALIGNMENT

CCW = LAMP INTQ REFLECTOR
CW   = LAMP OUT OF REFLECTOR

CCW - BEAM DOWN
CW   - BEAM UP

The rear cap and alignment adjustments of a standard ellipsoidal.

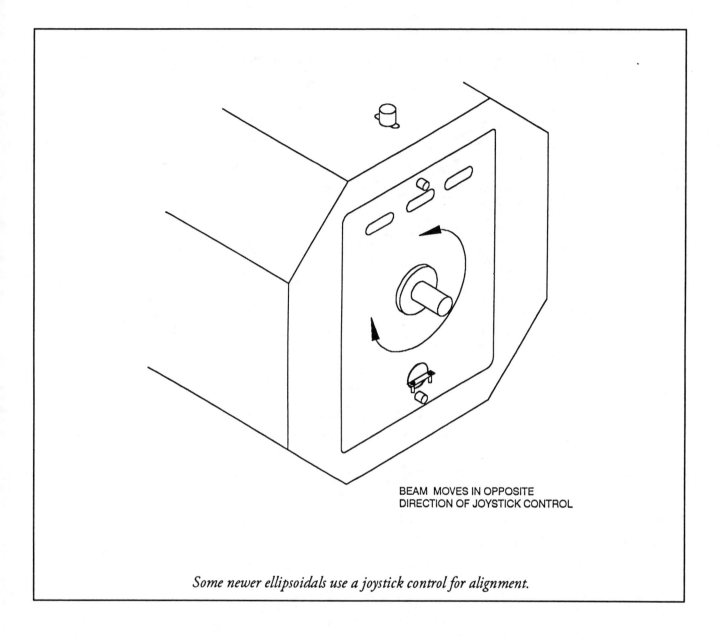

BEAM MOVES IN OPPOSITE
DIRECTION OF JOYSTICK CONTROL

Some newer ellipsoidals use a joystick control for alignment.

however. In many cases, the method of accessing the lamping requires the depth adjustment to be loosened and removed. This is a problem when a fast change needs to occur, and the fixture cannot be turned on to ensure proper realignment. Though each lamp is a little different, they are not so varied as to require a complete realignment with each lamp change.

The lenses are removed from the most common fixtures by removing the spring ring from the front of the instrument and sliding the lenses out. Other designs have lens access through a cover on the lens barrel or by removing the lens barrel. The lenses must be kept clean and free of fingerprints and oils. On many ellipsoidals, the "head" is common to all the different focal lengths. This allows converting from one to the other simply by changing the barrel and lenses.

Ellipsoidals should always travel and be stored with their shutters pushed in to prevent damage from bending or shearing off.

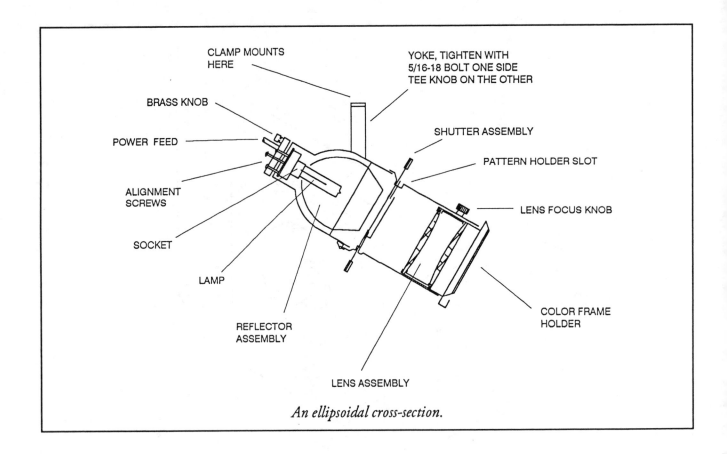

An ellipsoidal cross-section.

Standard 6-inch ellipsoidals use a 7½" x 7½" color-frame. The axial quartz instruments use a medium two-pin base, while the incandescent instruments use a medium prefocus base. The units weigh approximately 14 to 35 pounds, depending on design.

Fresnel Spotlights

Fresnels get their name from the type of lens used in the fixture. When you look at the fresnel lens you can see concentric rings cut into it. Since a fresnel has a controllable beam, it belongs to the group of instruments referred to as focusing instruments. The fresnel can be varied from a spot to a flood beam by changing the distance between the lamp and the lens. This is usually achieved by sliding the lamp forward or backward, though some units are being introduced with a fixed lamp and sliding lens. Each particular type of fresnel is named by the diameter of its lens, i.e., 3", 4½", 6", 8" ... The edge of the beam is always soft. There are many accessories that can be used with the fresnel spotlight to help control the beam a little more. The most popular types are the barn door and the funnel. Both are used to control the beam spread.

USES AND FOCUSING

Fresnels are primarily used for general color washes. Another common use is to create a low sidelight or backlight silhouette by mounting the units on the floor. The most popular fresnels are the 6-inch and the 8-inch. These two units are used in the same manner, the only difference being their size and the lamp used. To focus these units you either slide the screw located on the bottom of the unit forward for flood and back for spot, or turn the handle located at the back of the instrument counterclockwise for flood and clockwise for spot, depending on whether you have a slide focus or screw feed focus instrument.

RELAMPING

Relamping is carried out by opening the lens holder (remove the colorframe first or it may drop out) by either pulling up on or unscrewing the knob located on the lens holder, pulling the lens holder out, and letting it swing away. You then push gently down on the lamp and turn the lamp counterclockwise to line up the blades on the lamp with the openings in the socket, and pull the lamp out. To insert a new lamp, reverse the process. The lens is removed by removing the spring ring from the front of the instrument.

SPECIFICATIONS

6-Inch Fresnel

Medium prefocus socket
7½" x 7½" colorframe
120V T20 medium prefocus lamp or quartz retrofit
Weight approximately 7 lbs.

8-Inch Fresnel

Mogul prefocus socket
10" x 10" colorframe
120V G40 mogul prefocus lamp or quartz retrofit
Weight approximately 15 lbs.

Fresnel spotlights. Courtesy Lighting & Electronics.

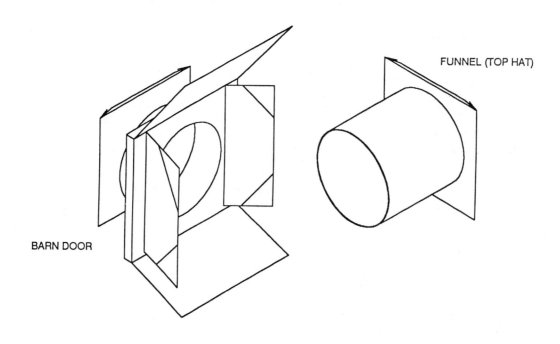

FUNNEL (TOP HAT)

BARN DOOR

Barn doors and top hats (funnels) are used to control the beam of various flood-type fixtures.

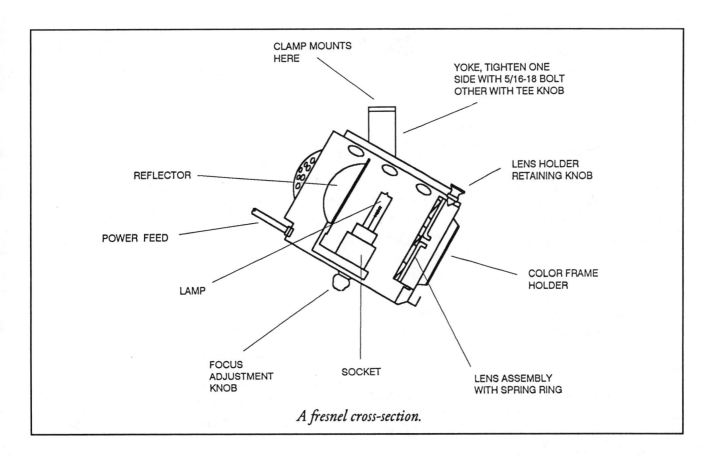

A fresnel cross-section.

Scoops

A scoop is basically a reflector ("scoop"-shaped) that floods light in a particular direction. Scoops do not offer much control over the light they produce but deliver a very even wash in the direction they are pointed. Each different kind is called out by the size of the eflector it incorporates, such as 10-inch, 14-inch, and 18-inch. You would usually find the scoop being used for lighting backgrounds and for even color washes across a stage. With beam spread factors ranging from 2 to 3.8, they provide very wide, even washes and are a practical way to get full stage washes with a minimum number of lighting instruments.

RELAMPING

Scoops are relamped by reaching into the front of the instrument and either unscrewing the lamp (in the case of the 10-inch, 14-inch, and 18-inch) or pressing the lamp slightly into the socket and turning it counterclockwise so the two blades on the lamp match the openings on the socket (14-inch focusing). The colorframe holders on scoops usually rotate 360°, so that the instrument can be hung at almost any position the lamp being used will allow.

SPECIFICATIONS

10-Inch Scoop

Medium screw socket
10½" x 10½" colorframe
Any 120V G30 lamp, medium screw base lamp

14-Inch Scoop

Mogul screw socket
15⅝" x 15⅝" colorframe
Any 120V PS52, mogul screw base lamp

14-Inch Focusing Scoop

Medium prefocus socket
15⅝" x 15⅝" colorframe
Any 120V T12 medium prefocus base lamp or quartz retrofit

18-Inch Scoop

Mogul screw socket
18" diameter colorframe
Any 120V PS52, mogul screw base lamp

Scoops and floods. Courtesy Lighting & Electronics.

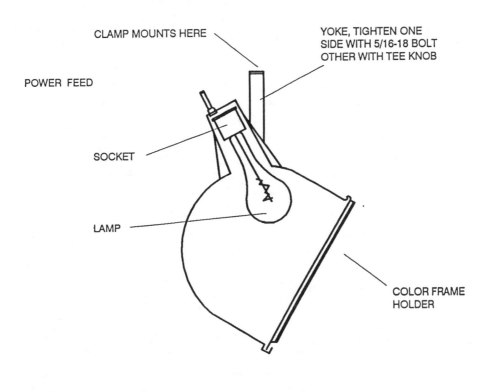

CLAMP MOUNTS HERE

YOKE, TIGHTEN ONE
SIDE WITH 5/16-18 BOLT
OTHER WITH TEE KNOB

POWER FEED

SOCKET

LAMP

COLOR FRAME
HOLDER

A scoop cross-section.

Striplights

The most common use for striplights is backdrop or cyclorama lighting. Striplights are used extensively for this purpose in all forms of stage lighting. They are also used for general stage washes, mostly in the form of down lights.

Striplights are just what the name implies, a strip of lights in one housing. There are many different kinds of striplight. There are strips that use regular "A" type lamps screwed into a reflector, ones that use "R" type flood lamps or PAR lamps, others that utilize double-ended T3 lamps, and some units that use low voltage MR-16 lamps. Striplights are also referred to as *borders, borderlights*, and *x-rays*. Many of the striplights used for background lighting are also available in single light versions.

CIRCUITS

Within a striplight containing multiple lamp compartments there is generally more than one electrical circuit. The most common numbers of circuits are three or four. In most fixtures the circuits alternate (1-2-3-1-2-3 ... in three-circuit, 1-2-3-4-1-2-3-4 ... in four-circuit, etc.) from lamp compartment to lamp compartment throughout the length of the strip. It is important on what centers the lamps are located. This means the distance measured from the center of one lamp to the center of the next lamp. The reason this can be important is that with very narrow beam lamps, if the compartments are too far apart, there will be some drop-off in intensity between the beams of light projected by lamps in the same electrical circuit. Generally, the lamp centers given by manufacturers are between each immediate compartment, not the compartments of a circuit. You can determine the spacing between lamp compartments on a circuit by adding the distances covered in a sequence (i.e., on a three-circuit fixture with 6-inch centers, the lamps are 18 inches apart; 3 x 6 = 18).

Another concern in any fixture with a series circuit is to be sure not to mix lamps of different wattages in a

single electrical circuit. Uneven loading will put extra electrical stress on the lamps, resulting in premature burnout.

EFFECTS

When used for background lighting, the effect usually desired is to obtain as even a wash of light over the background as possible. This can be done by placing a row of strips on the ground aiming up, and by hanging another set above and aiming down. If the drop is very tall, you will usually find double rows of strips with spots in half of the units and floods in the other half. The units with the spot are focused on the farthest part of the drop from the light, and the floods are focused on the nearest part. Considering that you generally want to have at least three color circuits to allow the greatest control of blending colors on the background, a large number of fairly large capacity dimmers may have to be used.

The mini-strip has several advantages over other types of strips. By using the 12V MR-16 lamp in a series of ten lamps, the light output of 750 watts on a circuit using 75 watt lamps is equivalent to the light output of any other strip using two to three times as much power. The mini-strip need only be 8 to 12 inches away from the drop to obtain even coverage; other strips have to be placed between 36 and 96 inches away. Physically, the mini-strip is much smaller than other strips. A small cross-section allows some versions to be placed in the center of a piece of 14-inch truss. They are often hung vertically to deliver a curtain of side light.

Striplights are commonly used in 6-foot and 8-foot lengths, but are available in almost any length required. Some installations have striplights that are the width of the stage (continuous borders). This arrangement has the disadvantage of inflexibility. A series of portable borders could be moved wherever they are most needed for a particular show; the continuous version must stay where it is originally hung.

Striplights and cyc lights. Courtesy Lighting & Electronics.

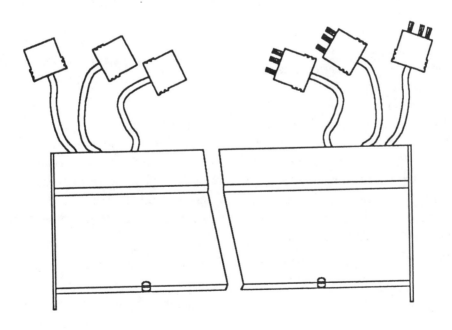

An R40 border with feed-through circuitry.

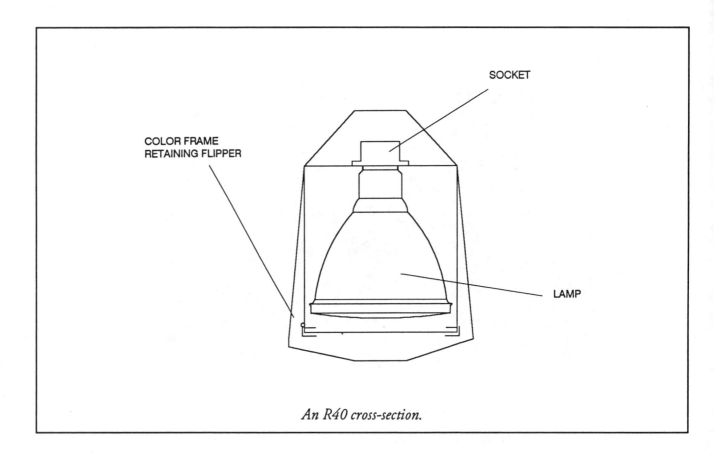

COLOR FRAME
RETAINING FLIPPER

SOCKET

LAMP

An R40 cross-section.

RELAMPING

R40 borders and A borders are relamped from the front by unscrewing their lamps from their sockets. The A borders should have their reflectors cleaned periodically. Most A borders can be transformed into R40 borders by loosening the two screws inside the reflector, turning it to position the screws inside the round part of the mounting slot, and pulling the reflector out of the unit. By using R40 lamps with their built-in reflectors (instead of A lamps inside the reflectors built into the border), you will generally be able to get more light out of the same wattage lamp, due to the better reflective surface and filament alignment in the R40 lamp. The borders are gelled by lifting the spring-hinged flippers and dropping the color frames, containing either glass *roundels* or plastic gel, into the color frame slot.

Cyc strips using the double-ended T3 lamp are relamped from the front by applying outward pressure on the spring-loaded sockets and removing the lamp. As with any fixture containing reflectors, the cyc strip should have its reflectors cleaned periodically to maintain optimum reflectivity. The cyc strip is gelled by opening one of the spring-loaded flippers (unlike most strips the cyc strip has flippers on both sides) and dropping the color frame into the slot.

PAR 56 and PAR 64 borders are relamped from the front by releasing the lamp, using a spring clip inside the lamp compartment, and then removing the lamp from the socket. The borders are gelled by lifting the spring-hinged flippers and dropping the color frames, containing either glass roundels (PAR 56 only) or plastic gel, into the color frame slots.

The mini-strip is relamped from the top by opening the lamp compartment door (releasing the spring latches to do so), pushing the lamp release lever, and pulling the lamp out of the socket. Mini-strips are gelled by lifting the spring-hinged flippers and dropping the color frames into the color frame slots. The lamp bars inside can be repositioned by loosening a set of screws either inside the unit or beneath the unit and moving the lamp bars to their next position. The bars are repositioned to keep the second focus point of the lamps (which is a point of light) off the gel. If the light is allowed to focus as a small point on the gel, the gel will burn out quite rapidly.

SPECIFICATIONS

R40 Border

Medium screw base socket
5¾" x 5¾" color frame
Any 120V R40 or PAR 38 lamp with a medium screw base
Lamps on 6-inch centers

A Border

Medium screw base socket
5¾" x 5¾" color frame
Any 120V A19 or A21 lamp with a medium screw base
Lamps on 6-inch centers

Cyc Strip

Recessed single contact socket (two per lamp)
12¾" x 8⅞" color frame
Any 120V 4 ¹¹⁄₁₆" MOL double-ended T3 lamp
Lamps on 9-inch centers

Mini-Strip

Rim mount two-pin socket
3⅞" x 4⁵⁄₁₆" color frame
Any 120V MR-16 lamp (up to 75W) with RM2P (GX5.3) base

Lamp compartments on 5-inch centers, each compartment contains two lamps (five compartments per circuit)

PAR 56 Border

Mogul end prong socket
7¾" x 7¾" color frame
Any 120V PAR 56 lamp with mogul end prong base
Lamps on 8-inch centers

PAR 64 Border

Mogul end prong socket
8¾" x 8¾" color frame
Any 120V PAR 64 lamp with mogul end prong base
Lamps on 9-inch centers

Followspots

One fixture that can add greatly to the finished look of a musical performance is the followspot. Followspots are used to allow a performer the freedom to move anywhere on stage while remaining in his own "special." Without a followspot a performer can only be highlighted by standing in a specific place where a fixture is focused. His movement is controlled by a motionless, static fixture. If a show is to retain the spontaneity that is expected, the performer must either remain in one basic area and a feeling of energy and movement must be created around that area, or many specials must be set with careful rehearsal to make the light appear to follow the performer, or a followspot must be used.

There are currently many different types of followspots on the market and so many new followspots appearing almost daily (due to rapid advancement in design of followspots), that justice cannot be done to them in a book of this nature. What can be done is to point out the main parameters to be considered when choosing or using a followspot.

PURCHASING CONSIDERATIONS

The first two things to consider are throw distance and budget. These points are unfortunately tied closely together. Followspots can be expensive, and they tend to get much more expensive in proportion to the distance of throw they can cover. You should not guess at the distance you will need to have your spot throw because inaccuracy could cause you to buy a spot too powerful for your needs. There could be a difference of as much as $1500. There is a large gap when you get to the 80' to 100' range. This is where you jump from the 1000W Quartz followspot to the Marc 350, HMI, and HTI followspots that can be substantially more expensive. Xenon followspots, the brightest design currently available, are considerably more expensive than the previously mentioned types.

IS A FOLLOWSPOT FOR YOU?

After you determine your throw distance and your budget you can decide whether you should incorporate a followspot into your show. If you cannot afford a followspot powerful enough for you, do not buy a less powerful one just to have a followspot. It is better to use focused specials that are powerful than a weak followspot that cannot cut through the rest of your stage lighting without making the stage very dim first.

You can determine if a followspot will do the job for you by checking how many footcandles it should deliver at the distance you intend to use it. Then figure out how bright the rest of the stage lighting is going to be when you intend to use the followspot. If the followspot is not approximately 70% or more as bright as the rest of the stage, you probably will not want to use it. If you want the followspot to make the person spotted really glow, you should go for an even larger difference either by using a brighter spot or a much paler color in the spot than on the stage. When looking at the footcandle performance to determine whether the unit will be bright enough, make sure the spot will deliver what it claims.

CONTROLLING THE BEAM

A followspot should give you the ability to control the beam it produces in a number of ways. The first requirement is that the spot be able to be adjusted on its stand and that it move up, down, and side to side easily, or you will not be able to follow someone smoothly. There should be an iris to allow you to make the beam larger or smaller while remaining round. You may also need some method of changing colors, as well as the ability to shut off the beam both gradually and rapidly. You will need the capacity to create a hard or soft edge on the beam. All these features are fairly standard on all followspots. What differs is how they are achieved.

Followspot for medium throw applications — 75- to 175-foot throws. Courtesy Lycian Stage Lighting.

Followspot for long throw applications — 150-foot or more throws. Courtesy Lycian Stage Lighting.

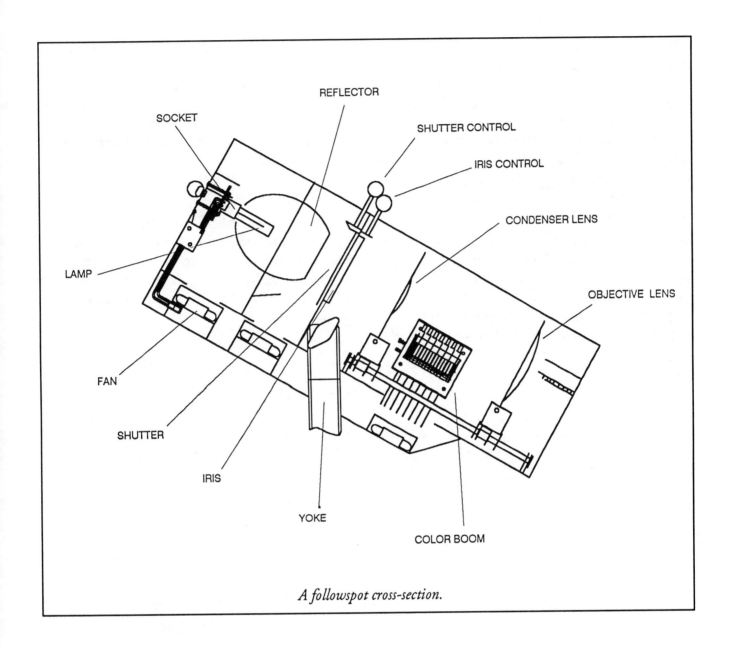

A followspot cross-section.

OPERATING A FOLLOWSPOT

When you are ready to purchase a followspot and are checking them out it is a good idea to actually operate one, if possible. Adjust the stand so that the height is comfortable for you. Is the spot still stable? Move the beam around. Can you create a fluid motion? Can you reach the colorchanger while operating the other controls? Can you adjust the iris while following someone with the beam? Is the method of blacking out the beam effective, and is it easy to do a slow fade? If you cannot operate the followspot effectively, it is going to cause problems when you try to use it in performance.

Look at the focusing system. Can you adjust one or more of the lenses? If you can adjust more than one you will be able to achieve as many different focus (hard-edge) points as the number of lenses you can adjust. There is a different photometric performance for each focus point you can achieve on the spot. Usually, as the beam diameter gets narrower when you adjust the lenses (not the iris), the beam will get brighter. If you have the specification sheet on the followspot you should find photometric data for different focus points (only if you can adjust more than one lens). Where it says "spot and flood," it is referring to the lens focus, not the iris position. If the spot can only adjust one lens and there is more than one set of photometric data (such as spot and flood focus), you should ask to be shown how these are achieved on the unit. They may be only theoretical or may even have been eliminated when there was a design change.

When you start using the followspot in a show, there are certain things that should be learned by the spot operator or he could ruin the look you are trying to create. When the spot is turned on it should be on the performer being spotted. If the spot is constantly missing and searching it will be very distracting. The spot should only move if the person it is on is moving. Basically the spot should move as if it were attached to the performer; if it is not in coordination with the performer, then it is stealing focus from the performer. If you remember the quality of light called movement you should be aware that it can work against you as well as for you.

MAINTENANCE

Look at how easy it will be to maintain the followspot. Since the lenses and reflector require periodic cleaning, how easy is it to remove them? How simple is the process of replacing the iris, something that will eventually become necessary. Are all parts of the fixture accessible?

Wiring Devices

The equipment used to carry the electricity from the dimmers to the lighting fixtures falls under the grouping referred to as *wiring devices*. There are a large number of wiring device types. Permanent installations often have a combination of several different kinds, connector strips, plug boxes (wall or pipe mounted), and floor pockets. Traveling shows generally either use the devices in the theater or club they are performing in, if they are set up for their use, or carry some portable devices (or both). These include jumper cables of various design and pipe-mounted plug boxes.

CONNECTOR STRIP

A connector strip is a wireway, most often extending the full width of the stage, hanging from the grid or ceiling, containing a number of receptacles tied into different electrical circuits. They can be very convenient if their circuitry is laid out to allow a lot of flexibility in the different designs that will hang in the theater or club. It is more common, unfortunately, for them to be laid out very inflexibly, with a particular lighting setup or hang in mind. Any changes will then put the circuitry in positions requiring a large number of jumper cables to be run. A flexible concept for setting up a permanent stage system is to utilize a number of pipe mount plug boxes set up as drop boxes. This allows the plug boxes to be relocated where they are needed during different lighting setups.

PLUG BOX

A plug box is exactly what it sounds like — a box containing one or more connectors for plugging fixtures into different electrical circuits. Plug boxes are commonly found with one to four connectors either flush-mounted in the box or at the ends of pigtails. It is generally a good idea to use flush receptacles in plug boxes since you often will have to use a jumper of some length anyway, and flush receptacles allow for a cleaner hang when some circuits go unused. Flush connectors also tend to hold up better and are easier to maintain. The connectors can be on either separate or shared circuits. It is rare to find a plug box containing more than six connectors. Surface-mounted boxes are permanently attached to the walls or ceiling of the stage. Recessed boxes are actually mounted into the walls or ceilings. Pipe mount boxes are attached to the battens or pipes off which the lighting fixtures are to be hung. If the pipe mount box is allowed enough cable and a mounting method that permits it to be relocated or stored at the ceiling or rid of the stage, it is referred to as a *drop box* since it can be dropped wherever it is needed.

FLOOR POCKET

Floor pockets are a variation of a recessed plug box used in the floor of the stage. A floor pocket always has a hinged door to allow people and settings to pass over it without falling in. Their use is not as common as it used to be. They can be convenient for lighting practicals (lights found in or mounted to the setting) or floor-mounted borders. Unfortunately, they often find themselves under the setting or props, out of reach to the electrician. Sometimes their covers break when an individual castor on a heavy set piece lands on top of them. A floor pocket may accidentally open, creating an extreme hazard for the performers and stagehands. Floor pockets are found with from one to four connectors, always flush, wired either together or on separate circuits.

SAFETY

It should be noted that it is an accepted rule, and an intelligent one, that the feed or line supplying the electrical power is *always* capped with a female connector. This eliminates the danger of live electrical parts being left exposed when a circuit is on but nothing is plugged into it, as would be the case if a male plug were supplying the electricity. There is no reason ever to deviate from this rule. The female connector supplies the power, the male plug accepts it.

Wiring devices. Courtesy Lighting & Electronics.

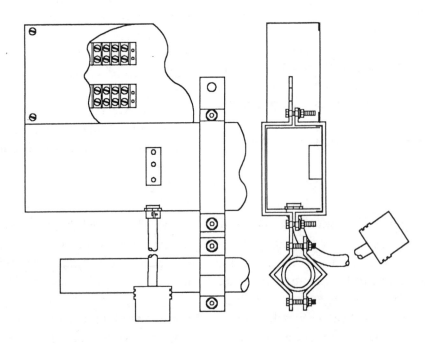

A connector strip upstage view and cross-section.

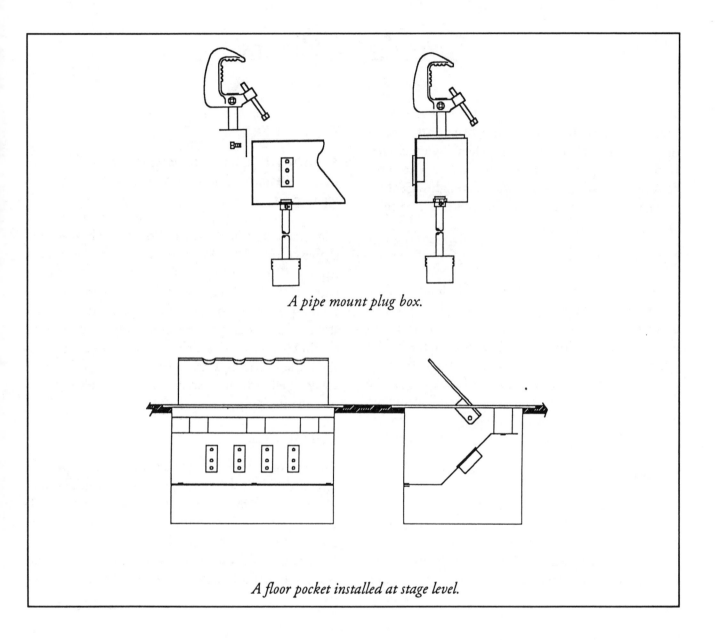

A pipe mount plug box.

A floor pocket installed at stage level.

In the section on electricity the idea of ampacity of cable is mentioned. This is an important concept to understand. Wiring devices (cables, connectors, plug boxes, connector strips, input leads on a lighting fixture, etc.) have a limit to how much current — amperage — they can carry. If you exceed the ampacity limits of an electrical device it will fail. If you are lucky it will just stop working or trip a breaker. If any safety components such as fuses or circuit breakers connected to a wiring device or cable have a higher rating than the wiring device itself, too much current will flow through the device, causing it to burn up, possibly taking the stage and anyone on it with it. Read the section on electricity carefully so that you will be better able to avoid a potentially hazardous situation.

Special Effects

Only the effects used with the lighting instruments discussed in this book are covered here. Pyrotechnics, lasers, and fog effects are not included. The most common special effects used with stage lighting equipment are colorwheels, mirrorballs, patterns, and color changers.

COLORWHEELS

A colorwheel mounts in the colorframe holder on the instrument that is going to light through it. Fresnels and ellipsoidals are most commonly used, although any instrument with a 7½" x 7½" colorframe holder will work. The effect is of slow, constantly changing colors. Colorwheels have often been used to create the effect of a distant fire or water, depending on the colors chosen. Most wheels have five or six holes that can be gelled any color you wish.

MIRRORBALLS

The mirrorball is a classic effect that gained its popularity during the golden era of ballroom dancing. It has become a standard on dance floors and in slow musical numbers, creating a dreamlike vision of floating stars. Mirrorballs are now available in almost any shape and size.

PATTERNS

A pattern is a silhouette projected from an ellipsoidal. In the theater and music industries they are often referred to as *gobos*. A large variety of off-the-shelf patterns is available. They come in designs from realistic scenes and objects to abstract and biomorphic shapes. Custom-made patterns can also be created from your own artwork. You can make your own patterns if you wish from almost any sheet metal — even a pie tin can be used for simple patterns. You should realize that patterns eventually burn up from the intense heat to which they are subjected. You should have backups ready. The section of the book covering ellipsoidals describes how to install a pattern into the instrument.

COLOR CHANGERS

Color changers are devices that enable you to preload several different gel colors onto an instrument and change them remotely during a show. They are available in a variety of styles and designs. The effect can be quite dramatic if they are fast, accurate, and quiet. They can also cut down on the amount of instrumentation required, though they tend to be quite expensive.

Electricity

CAUTION: Electricity can be extremely dangerous; do not try to make connections with which you are not familiar. Consult a qualified technician about hookups and tie-ins. Additional information may be obtained by consulting National Electrical Code texts.

When dealing with stage lighting, there are three components of electricity you should be familiar with: volts, amps, and watts.

VOLTAGE

Voltage (measured in volts - V) is the difference in charge between the most negative point and the most positive point of a circuit. Normally, this means the difference between ground (or neutral) and the "hot" line. Typical household voltage in the United States is 120V AC (alternating current). This is probably the only voltage you will need to be concerned with, unless you plan to travel to other countries where different voltages are common, or you plan to measure the output signals of your control equipment, where you would find low voltage direct current (DC). You would also run into higher voltages if you intend to "tie in" to a main power distribution panel to get your power. Under these circumstances you need to be concerned with what phase your dimmers are wired in. Phase is symbolized as ø, and common examples are 3ø208V with three "hot" legs (red, black, and blue), neutral (white), and ground (green); 1ø120V with one "hot" leg (black), neutral (white), and ground (green) — this last is standard house voltage. If you are going to be dealing with electricity, you should seek the advice of a qualified electrician to learn about the different configurations you may encounter.

AMPERAGE

Amperage (measured in amps - A) is the number of electrons (the negatively charged part of an atom) moving past a given point within a given time period. Amperage is also known as electric current. Amperage

ratings are commonly found on fuses, plugs and receptacles, circuit breakers, and dimmers. The average household circuit breaker is 15 to 20 amps rated. Under continuous loads, defined in the National Electrical Code as when components on a circuit are on for three hours or more, it is a general rule to derate cable ampacities (maximum amperage carried by a cable) by twenty percent. This means if a constant load is placed on a circuit you multiply any amperage capacities of the wiring by 0.8 to determine the continuous duty capacity. The average performance would fall far short of being considered continuous duty.

WATTAGE

Wattage or power (measured in watts - W) is the total amount of energy consumed by a circuit. One watt of power is consumed when one volt pushes one ampere through a circuit. Lamps are generally rated in watts to reflect the power they consume when they are placed in a circuit. For convenience, dimmers are often rated by the maximum wattage they can handle so that you need only total the wattage of the lamps you intend to plug into a dimmer to check if you are within its capacity. Some manufacturers do rate their dimmers by amperage; in those cases you would have to convert from wattage to amperage to check if your load (lamps in the circuit) is within capacity.

CONVERSION BETWEEN UNITS

You need to be concerned with the relationship of the three components. This relationship can be expressed by the equation Watts = Volts x Amps (in engineering, $P = EI$ where P = power (watts), E = voltage, I = amperage). It is important for you to understand this equation since it can make your design and setup much easier when determining dimmer assignments and how large an electrical service you will require. A popular method used to remember this equation is to use the abbreviation for West Virginia, WVa (W = V x A).

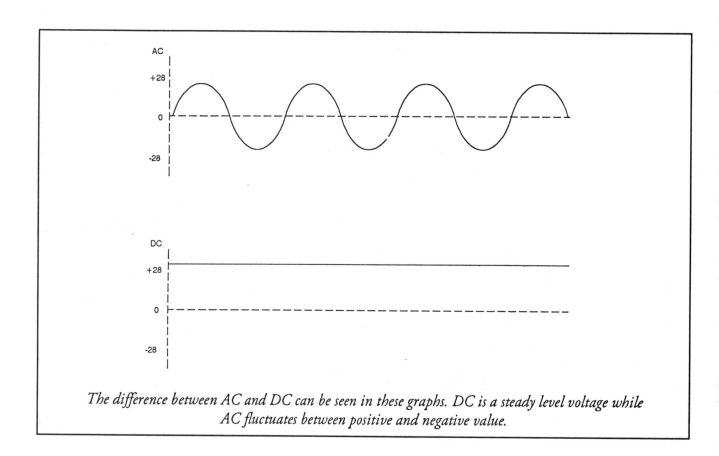

The difference between AC and DC can be seen in these graphs. DC is a steady level voltage while AC fluctuates between positive and negative value.

EXAMPLE 1: You have 24 PAR 64's in a light plot, 16 with 1000W lamps and 8 with 500W lamps. Your total wattage is 20,000 watts. W = V x A can be rearranged to be A = W/V or A = 20,000/120 or A = 166.67

You will need at least 167 amps available.

EXAMPLE 2: You only have 18-gauge cables (rated for 10 amps max under temporary loads), and you want to have eight 300W PAR56 lamps on one dimmer. How many lamps can you have on one cable? W = V x A, total wattage for 18 gauge would be determined by 120V x 10A = 1200W. Therefore you can only put four lamps on one cable if you wish to bring it to the maximum rating (which is *not* a good idea).

Amperage Requirements for Dimmers

To determine service required, divide amps by number of hot legs in service:

6 — 2.4K dimmers (20A)

    20A x 6 = 120A total service required

3ø4 wire & gnd	40A/hot leg
1ø3 wire & gnd	60A/hot leg
1ø2 wire & gnd	120A on hot leg

6 — 3.0K dimmers (25A)

    25A x 6 = 150A total service required

3ø4 wire & gnd	50A/hot leg
1ø3 wire & gnd	75A/hot leg
1ø2 wire & gnd	150A on hot leg

3ø4 wire & gnd

    3 hot legs, 1 neutral leg, 1 ground wire

    normally red, black, blue for hot

    white for neutral

    green for ground

1ø3 wire & gnd

    2 hot legs, 1 neutral leg, 1 ground wire

    normally red, black for hot

    white for neutral

    green for ground

1ø2 wire & gnd

    1 hot leg, 1 neutral leg, 1 ground wire

    normally black for hot

    white for neutral

    green for ground

1ø2 wire is common house wiring and not recommended for hookup of most dimmers. Most often the service coming into the building is 1ø3 wire or 3ø4 wire and breaks down to 1ø2 wire in the electric panels. A trained electrician can do a dimmer tie-in before the electric panels break down the phases.

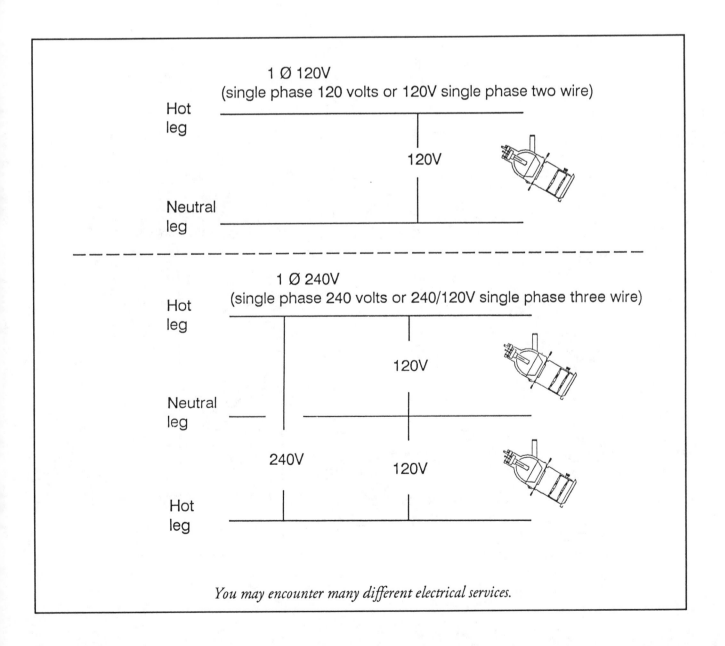

You may encounter many different electrical services.

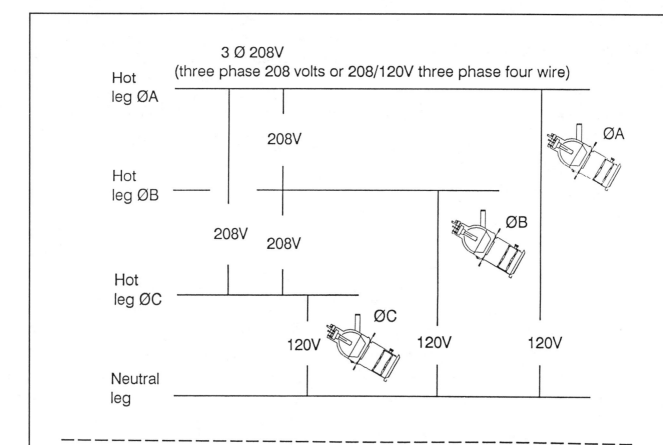

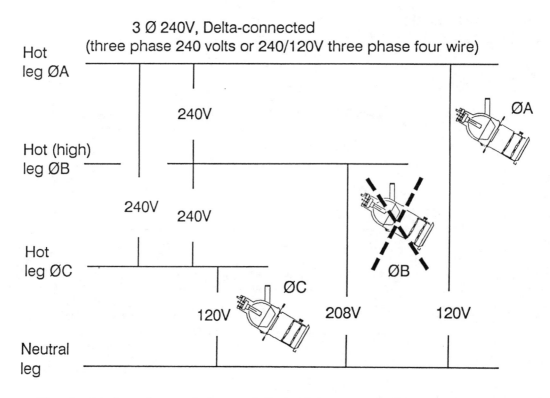

You should always know which type of electrical service you will have to deal with.

Control

Without some form of control, your lights can provide little more than visibility. Though there are many forms of control available, they all provide the same basic functions:

1. They supply electric power for the lighting fixtures.
2. They allow the ability to limit the electric power to the lighting fixtures.

The complexity of control comes from the methods used and versatility allowed in providing the two functions of control.

The most basic form of control is the simple electric switch on an electric cord (feeder cable). With the cable plugged into an electrical outlet and a lighting instrument plugged into the cable, the function of providing power is furnished. The switch supplies the most basic form of limiting — on and off. The next step is to use a dimmer instead of a switch. This extends the range of limiting to include everything in between on and off. A bank of dimmers could be used to control a number of instruments. By setting each light at various levels, a variety of looks or scenes could be created. Add a single "master" dimmer to dim all the individual dimmers together without changing their relative settings, and you can "preset" a scene before turning on any lights and then change the mood by dimming them all together. Next, add a second bank of dimmers that controls the same fixtures so you can set a scene on one bank while the other bank is on and then switch back and forth while changing the settings. This is a simple explanation of what has been happening to stage lighting control over the years, culminating with the new state-of-the-art digital dimmers controlled by computerized control boards, outputting multiplexed, digital, low voltage control signals.

When looking into purchasing, renting, or using control equipment there are certain terms that should be understood. The following are some you should know:

BLACKOUT SWITCH — Instantly turns everything off for effective blackouts.

BUMP BUTTON — Button that momentarily flashes everything on a channel to full on. (Some boards also allow the momentary dropping to full off with the bump button.)

CHASE CONTROL — Allows the "chasing" of two or more channels. This refers to the rapid switching of channels on and off in sequence (1-2-1-2-1 ... or 1-2-3-1-2-3-1 ...) to give the illusion that the lights are chasing each other. When the fixtures on the chase are not placed in any particular order a very random effect can be produced, which is effective for simulating explosions and lightning.

CIRCUIT — The cable or outlet into which you plug the fixture. The circuit is then plugged into a dimmer. More than one circuit can be plugged into one dimmer, providing that the dimmer's maximum power capacity (wattage) is not exceeded.

CONTROL BOARD — The unit the operator manipulates to control how much power the dimmer supplies to the lighting fixture.

CONTROL CABLE — The cable that carries the signal between the control board and the dimmers.

CONTROL CHANNEL — Anything controlled by a specific potentiometer on a control board. This can be a single dimmer or (in the case of a computer board) a large number of dimmers "patched" together. To avoid confusion it is best always to refer to the control on the board as a channel, not a dimmer.

CONTROL PATCH — Assignment of a dimmer to a specific control channel. This is often one-to-one unless done with a computerized or semi-computerized control board, in which case dimmers may be ganged together in one channel (this is often referred to as a *soft* patch).

CONTROL SIGNAL — The voltage signal sent from the control board to the dimmer to determine the level at which it is to operate. The most common control signal has a range of one to ten volts DC (direct current).

CROSS FADER — Potentiometer that allows for the smooth switching between preset scenes. You should always look for a "dipless" fader, otherwise you can experience a slight darkening on stage as you switch scenes, which is not acceptable.

DIMMER — The electronic device that supplies power to the lighting fixture at varied magnitudes. Dimmers are usually grouped in packs or banks.

GRAND MASTER — The potentiometer that controls the level of all channels in all presets.

INDEPENDENT SWITCH — Takes a channel off the scene master, allowing it to be controlled independently of other channels.

LOAD — The lighting fixtures placed on a circuit are the loads on the circuit; the circuits placed in the dimmer are the loads on the dimmer; the dimmers placed in the control channel are the loads on the control channels ... You should try to avoid loading a circuit or dimmer to its maximum. This way you will be less likely to lose a circuit or dimmer to fast on's and such. As a rule, you should avoid loading a dimmer beyond 80% of its maximum capacity.

PATCH — Generally refers to patching circuits into dimmers. This is carried out by either actually plugging the various circuits directly into each dimmer, or with a patch panel in which leads (or sliders) representing specific circuits are plugged into receptacles (or slid onto busses) that are connected to specific dimmers. The most flexible patch is when every circuit has its own dimmer or "dimmer per circuit." This, in effect, makes every fixture a special. It does become more difficult to run a show if too many control channels need be manipulated quickly, which is why soft patching and computer boards are necessary when shows become quite large.

POTENTIOMETER (or POT) — Each individual control on the control board. There is usually a scale to allow presetting levels (usually 1-10, which is just a reference and does not indicate the control signal voltage level).

PRESET — To set up dimmer levels prior to making the setup active.

PRESET SCENE — The group of pots on the board that work together for presetting one "scene" of all the control channels. Boards are available with one, two, three, four, five or more scenes, though more than five is rare and two is the most common. They are usually labeled A, B, C ... or X, Y in a two-scene preset board. On a computerized board, the presets are done once and recorded on some form of magnetic media, such as a disk or cassette. Then they are read into memory shortly before they are needed.

SCENE MASTER — The potentiometer that controls the level of all the channels in one preset scene.

SPLIT FADER — A version of a cross fader allowing you to add one preset scene to another, as well as simple cross fading. When you add a scene on top of another, if a channel is at a given level in both it will be brought to the higher of the two. The two settings are not added together, and it does not matter which scene contains the higher level.

TIE-IN — The act of connecting a portable dimming system to a building's power distribution system. This should not be attempted by anyone without proper training, as it can be extremely dangerous if improperly done.

There are four basic components to a control system — the control board, the control cable, the dimmer, and the patching device. Circuit cabling is not included in the list because it is part of the distribution system, not the control system. The distribution system is the wiring between the control system and the lighting fixtures themselves.

CONTROL BOARD

The control board is the front end of the system. It can be as simple as a small panel of individual dimmers or switches or as complex as a top-of-the-line, state-of-the-art computer board. There are three designs of control board most commonly found in use now: the preset board, the computerized preset board, and the computer board. Prior to these designs dimmer boards consisted of a number of large levers that were part of

Preset control board. Courtesy Electronics Diversified.

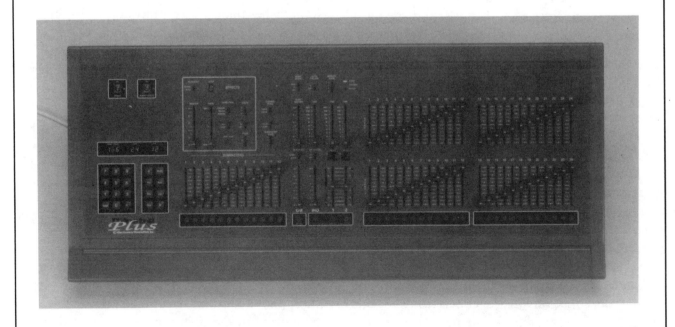

Computer preset control board. Courtesy Electronics Diversified.

the actual dimmers. These were often referred to as piano boards. A lever for each dimmer was required. With this design it was so difficult for one person to reach and change more than a couple of dimmers at a time that several operators were needed for even moderately complex cues. You had to move each lever when the lighting change was desired. Because of the large size of the dimmers and the means available for changing the dimmer settings, lighting designs had to be kept fairly simple if they were to be executed at all. All boards used today are remote control boards, sending some form of control signal to the dimmers.

Preset Board

The preset board is the simplest kind used today. It is set up with a number of banks of pots (potentiometers) for adjusting the levels on the individual control channels. The pots have a scale, usually from one to ten, marked next to them to allow consistent settings of the levels for each control channel. Each bank of pots is referred to as a *preset scene* and is identical to the other banks on the board. There are generally from one to five presets on a board, each with from six to forty-eight channels. There are boards available with more channels, but it becomes very difficult to change a preset in the time usually available when you exceed forty-eight channels. At that point a computer board of some design should be considered.

The most commonly used design of preset board has two presets and is referred to as a two-scene preset. Preset boards usually have a grand master available for fading all the presets currently active, as well as a grand blackout switch. Preset boards also have some kind of cross fader whose purpose is to fade from one preset bank to the next. A special form of cross fader, called the *split fader*, is used both to fade between presets and to pile one preset on top of the other. You will also often find a series of switches, called *independent switches*, that allows an individual channel to be controlled independently from the rest of the channels, regardless of the setting of the preset masters. The general concept behind these boards is that while one preset is on, or active, the other or others can have the next cue or cues preset on them. As the next preset is made active, by cross fading into it, the previous one is cleared and reset for another cue. With careful

planning and attentive operation a show can move through its cues with major changes occurring evenly and smoothly.

On large shows, using large numbers of channels and presets, it is common to have two operators, the preset operator and the control operator. Their individual responsibilities are pointed out by their titles.

One aspect of running a preset board that can be either an advantage or a disadvantage is that the operator is solely responsible for the timing of cues. This is an advantage if you have a good operator. Live performances are dynamic. They can vary to a degree from performance to performance. The most common place this can be seen is in the timing of a show. If the performers are particularly up or down, the audience very responsive or nonexistent, the timing of the performance can be different from scene to scene. Because of this, the timing set up during the first weeks of a show is basically relative. The actual timing of a cue is most effective if it is a product of the show as it is being performed. Relative terms are used to describe cue timing, such as a fast fade to black, a slow fade up, etc. Cross fades are to be carried out in ten counts, the measure of which is based on the mood of the performance, much like the tempos of music. The actual timing, when under the control of a sensitive operator, can vary slightly to support the timing of the performance actually taking place, and thereby better present the lighting design as envisioned by the designer. It can add a subtle quality to a show that the audience will feel but never recognize. It is part of what is often referred to as the "spark" in a good performance. This flexibility in timing can be a disadvantage, granted a large disadvantage, if you do not have an operator who can "finesse" a show. Bad timing at the lighting control board can throw off a performance even more than good timing can enhance it. It can even affect the performers' timing to a large degree.

Of all the different control board designs available, the preset board is often the most convenient for houses whose shows must be set up quickly or allow some spontaneity to the performances. Houses that have one-night specials coming through are often better off with a preset board than a computer board since the shows are often created at the board. Many concerts

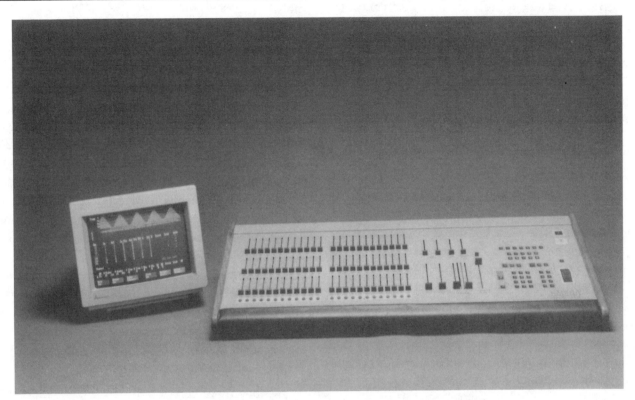

Computer control board. Courtesy Electronics Diversified.

Computer control board. Courtesy Electronics Diversified.

are better served by a preset board than a full computer board. The immediacy of the control and quick access to each channel are vital to some performances. The preset board is also generally the least expensive design available. Many very complex, visually exciting designs have been executed on a preset board, so don't underestimate its value.

Computerized Preset Board

The next step toward automation in lighting control is the computerized preset board. This design has many, often all, of the advantages of the preset board and many of those of the computer board. The basic layout of the computerized preset board is similar to that of the standard preset board. The board most often contains two presets, a cross fader, a grand master, and virtually all the controls found on a standard preset board. The differences in design are that one of the presets can be used to create small scenes and assign them to one of the channel controls. Many of the boards are available with soft patching.

The feature of scene assignment can be very handy in a show with some complex cues that come very fast. What is involved is first setting the levels of all the control channels to create a look or scene on stage as with the standard preset board, but then assigning the entire preset setup to a single pot on the board. After this is done, anytime you want to recreate the entire scene, all you need do is bring up the one pot. Many computerized preset boards have what is called *multiple pages*. This means each pot can have as many full scenes assigned to it as the board has pages. This feature allows a board containing thirty-six channels to hold a couple of hundred different scenes. Most computerized preset boards allow manual control of individual channels along with the use of pre-assigned scenes. This allows the operator to make immediate, real-time adjustments to a scene if it should prove necessary.

Computer Control Boards

Full-featured computer control boards are available in a variety of different designs. There are some common features found on most computer boards. Virtually all computer boards have soft patching. A common setup for a computer board is to have the capability of patching 999 dimmers into 120 control channels. Larger and smaller versions are available.

Every computer board must have some means of entering the patching and preset levels, referred to as *programming the show*. Some have a setup similar to a preset on a preset board on which you set the scene and transfer the setting to memory. This style is usually limited to the smaller channel capacity boards. The most common design has the capability of typing the setting into memory. This is done on either a standard computer-style keyboard or on a special keyboard with very specialized keys designed for the computer board. Many boards have a wheel that can be used for setting or modifying the levels of different channels. There is sometimes a wheel for controlling the rate at which a cue is carried out. Most of the boards with wheels allow the wheel to be activated to modify the recorded information during the show. This gives the operator the ability to make slight changes in timing if a particular performance requires it.

Many boards offer a few independent faders onto which you can program a full scene, much like on a computerized preset board. These are often used to set up a series of presets to be used in the event of main board failure. For this reason, it is important that the presets be set up independent of the main board. These faders often have several pages to allow more scenes to be recorded than there are faders. If you have this setup, be sure to program a backup show. You may never need it, but many people have and it has saved many performances and much anxiety having it all planned out ahead of time.

Computer boards have some form of monitor to allow you to view various pieces of information while programming and running a show. You can usually display the patching setup, any temporary reassignments, the current levels and timing, the next cue levels and timing, and blind programming.

On a computer board the level of each channel in a cue is recorded, along with the cue number, cue entry rate, and cue exit rate. The reason you enter both an entry rate and an exit rate is that with a computer board you are able to have the next cue come up at a different rate than the existing cue exits. This can be used to create some very interesting cross fade effects. The actual sequence for typing and recording both the patching setup and the cues for a show varies greatly from board to board. The operating manual for the particular board you are interested in should be referred to for specific procedures.

Generally, when you are programming a show you bring up the scene you are programming on stage so you can see what is happening. Sometimes there is something happening that will not allow you to do this, such as a show or rehearsal. At that time you can go into *blind mode*. In blind mode a cue is left up on stage, and you go to a new page that allows you to work on another cue without affecting the active one.

A very convenient feature on many computer boards is the ability to reassign a dimmer in the patch temporarily, or substitute a control channel for another throughout the entire show, by typing in a single entry. This becomes necessary when you lose a fixture or dimmer during a show and have to change the setup until it can be repaired.

All computer boards have some means of recording and backing up a show's program. Most often this is done on a floppy disk, though some still use a cassette tape. If you have a choice, opt for the disk; it is much faster and easier to store. A very smart practice is to back up your show more than once. It is generally recommended that you have several copies of a show besides the one in the board's memory. Keeping one out of the building, one in your office, and one in the drive of the board will cover most problems that can occur. Also keep the show documentation on file to allow easy retracing of a show setup should it prove necessary. As easy as it is to back up, there is no excuse for a show's suffering due to loss of a program.

Soft Patching vs. Patch Panels

Soft patching is an extremely versatile tool if the stage is set up for it. Dimmers are assigned to control channels on the board by typing the setup into the control on some form of keypad or with a low voltage patch panel using small jumpers. A number of dimmers can be ganged on an individual channel, allowing similar fixtures connected to several small capacity dimmers to be controlled by the same channel instead of having the fixtures plugged into one large capacity

High density dimmer rack.
Courtesy Electronics Diversified.

dimmer. With systems not having a soft patch capability, either a few large dimmers are used to control fixtures that need to work together, or more control channels are required to bring up all the smaller capacity dimmers at the same time. A patch panel or bay is used to patch different circuits into dimmers. The dimmers and control channels are set up in a one-to-one sequence so no control patching is used. The concept of the patch panel was discussed earlier in the definition section of this chapter. Patch panels are very expensive, and a soft patch system should be considered whenever possible. The cost of the extra dimmers required to create a system allowing effective control patching is often less expensive than a patch bay, and offers a significant increase in system flexibility. Aside from the question of economics, a soft patch system also gives the operator more immediate control of the patch should an emergency require an impromptu repatch.

Computerized preset boards are very popular for concerts. They allow the immediate access to control channels often desired along with the ability to program the major scenes equired throughout the concert for fast access to entire scenes. This board design, along with the standard preset board, is a good choice for theaters where fast show turnarounds are required, as well as for houses anticipating very complex designs. The cost of this type of board is higher than that of a standard preset board — unless choosing a standard board involves also buying a patch panel, in which case the computerized preset board with soft patch will prove considerably less expensive.

CONTROL SIGNALS

Whether a preset, computerized preset, or full computer board is to used, the choice between a digital or an analog control signal must be made. More and more people are moving toward the digital signal since it allows the control of many more dimmers with only one or two control cables being used. Analog systems generally need one cable for every six dimmers. This need for more control cables can actually work out to be an advantage since loss of a cable will only drop six dimmers on an analog system, whereas the whole digital system can be lost. A digital system can also be more sensitive to electrical "noise" or interference, resulting in garbled signals reaching the dimmers.

When deciding whether to use an analog or a digital system, it is important to make sure your control board and dimmer packs are talking the same language. Another disadvantage of the digital system is that not all systems use a standard signal. This means that one manufacturer's board may not be able to control another manufacturer's dimmers. There is, however, a standard analog signal, as well as cable connector, used on almost all boards and dimmers. Many digital control boards have a "magic box" available to translate their signal into analog. This allows a single cable to be run to the box and then separate cables to be run to each dimmer pack. Many rental houses supply both their control boards and dimmer packs set up for analog to better ensure compatibility. You would be wise to check what the shops in your area stock to allow for renting equipment from them in the event it proves necessary. Even if you are buying your own equipment, you may need to supplement it should you either have a larger show come in or experience equipment failure. Don't forget always to have a convenient source for backup equipment, just in case.

When you buy or rent a system of any design, always have an extra control cable available. The control cable is the weakest link in your system and the hardest to replace when you need it most. Run the extra when you set up. You will need it someday.

If you are working on a strict budget but intend to grow, it is a good idea to purchase a control board with more channels than you are buying dimmers. This generally is a relatively small increase in cost and allows you to add another bank of dimmers in the future without the full cost of a new board. You would also be able to rent an extra bank if you only occasionally need the extra dimmers.

OTHER PATCHES

When discussing computerized, or soft, patching, we were discussing patching dimmers to control channels on the control board. Another form of patch exists for patching the circuits into dimmers. There are a number

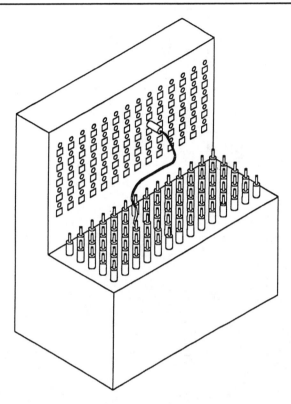

"Telephone" patch panels were very popular at one time. They are seldom supplied any more.

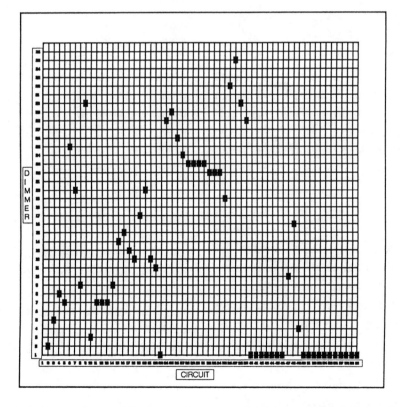

A slider patch panel is more convenient, though it can be quite costly.

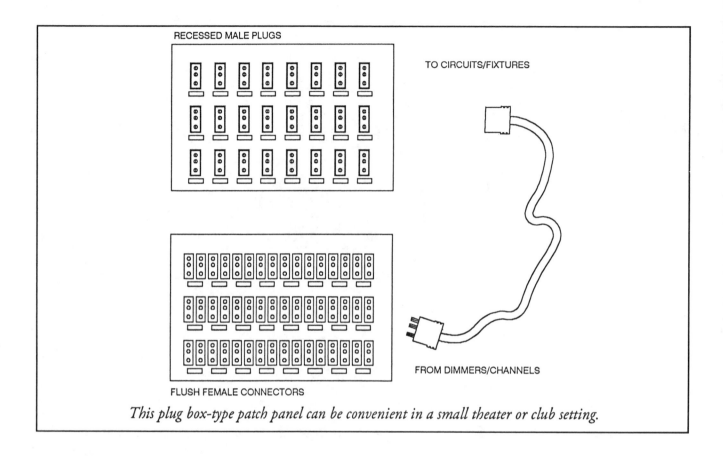

RECESSED MALE PLUGS

TO CIRCUITS/FIXTURES

FROM DIMMERS/CHANNELS

FLUSH FEMALE CONNECTORS

This plug box-type patch panel can be convenient in a small theater or club setting.

of ways this task can be carried out. The easiest is a dimmer per circuit patch. With this system, each circuit is always plugged into a particular dimmer. This is especially convenient if you also have soft patching to allow fixtures to be ganged together at the control board. More often there are more circuits than there are dimmers. In this case, you must be able to plug multiple circuits into the different dimmers.

One method used to patch circuits into dimmers is running cable jumpers from the circuit termination (either a breakout box of some design or another cable) to the dimmer of your choice. This is the most basic, and probably most used, form of dimmer/circuit patching. It works quite well if you keep things neat and organized. If this system is allowed to become a pile of tangled cable with no means of tracing any circuit path, nothing but trouble can come of it.

Another setup is to have two panels of connectors, one with female connectors tied into the dimmers, and one with male connectors tied into the circuits. Patch-

ing is carried out by jumping between the different circuit and dimmer connectors to tie the proper circuits and dimmers together. The older "telephone operator" style of patch panel falls in this design group. This kind of patching can be easier to keep organized than using just jumpers. A fairly large area must be allocated to it if a large number of circuits and dimmers are involved.

Another form of patch panel, or patch bay, is the cross connect slider system. This consists of a large matrix with dimmer numbers running up one side and circuit numbers running along the bottom. Each dimmer and circuit number is located on a slot going the full width or height of the panel. Each circuit has a slider in its slot that can be slid up the slot to stop at any dimmer slot. When this is done, the slider forms an electrical bridge between two copper busses, one attached to the dimmer and one to the circuit, effectively patching the circuit into the dimmer.

Dimmer pack. Courtesy Electronics Diversified.

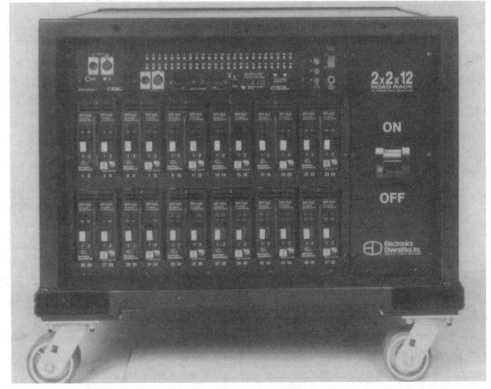

Portable dimmer pack. Courtesy Electronics Diversified.

AVOID HOT PATCHING
AND OVERLOADING

When using any form of patch, two practices must be avoided: hot patching and overloading. It is not good for any of the systems described to have the loads patched, or plugged, into the dimmer while the dimmer is on and its control channel is reading more than zero. This is referred to as *hot patching*. The arcing that results from this action will cause some damage, leading to eventual failure of the components of the patch system. Overloading is very easy when circuit patching if you do not have proper documentation as to what load is on each circuit. Accidentally patching too many fixtures onto one dimmer will result in activating the system's over-current protection.

Virtually all dimmers currently in use are based on using some form of silicon controlled rectifier (SCR) circuit as the heart of each module. The SCR dimmer has many advantages over older designs (resistance, autotransformer, thyratron, and magnetic amplifier). The SCR dimmer is smaller, having very high density racks containing 120 or more 20A dimmers in the same space once used to house twenty-four of the older design dimmers. SCR dimmers are less expensive to maintain, both through the use of inexpensive components and by having longer periods between repairs than the older designs. The circuits tend to run more quietly than the older dimmers, both audibly and electromagnetically (noise in amplifier circuits and such). The dimmers must contain the proper filtering circuitry to keep the noise down, but most dimmer manufacturers include such circuitry in their designs. One thing to be aware of when using the high density packs available (not all SCR packs are high density) is that due to the quantity of large capacity dimmers in a relatively small rack, fans are used to keep the components from overheating. These fans can be quite loud during a quiet scene or song. Any dimmer pack or rack having fans should be located far enough away from the stage, in another room if possible, so that the sound of the fans will not interfere with the performance. Fans are needed only because the dimmers are in a compact space. SCR style dimmers run cooler than older dimmers of similar capacity. The portable pack designs utilizing SCR circuitry are also generally lighter in weight than comparable packs using the earlier dimmer types.

All dimmers should have some form of over-current protection for each individual dimmer or module. These are either fuses or circuit breakers. Circuit breakers are fast becoming the standard since they are more convenient for the end user than fuses. If your dimmers are of the design using fuses, always make sure you have an ample supply of spare fuses of the correct size. It also doesn't hurt to have spare circuit breakers if your packs use them. As circuit breakers age they begin to fail under smaller loads and should be replaced. It is foolish to wait until you need new fuses or breakers to buy them. The delay could compromise your production for a very minor savings. You should never try to get around a fuse that continuously burns out by replacing it with one of higher capacity, or a breaker that trips by taping it on. Fuses and breakers blowing is a clear sign of equipment failure or overload. Bypassing the over-current protection in any way can lead to seriously damaging your equipment or starting a fire. If a fuse or breaker keeps blowing and there are not too many fixtures on the circuit and the load (fixtures and circuits on the dimmer) proves not to have any short circuits, it is a good idea either to switch the load to another dimmer to test how it holds or to replace the dimmer module so the one in question can be repaired. For this reason it is always wise to purchase one or two extra dimmer modules when you buy your dimmers. You will be able to replace the faulty module quickly and worry about it at a time when you are not faced with a performance.

Most dimmer packs are relatively easy to switch modules in. The majority of the newer designs allow the switch to occur by simply loosening a fastener, sliding the old module out of its track, and sliding the new module into the track and securing the fastener. No wiring need be handled. On older packs there may be a couple of wires that have to be removed to take out the old dimmer and installed to put in the new pack. Even these designs only require a couple of minutes to carry out the switch, since they almost always use terminal blocks with pressure-type screw terminals to attach the wires. You should familiarize yourself with the procedure required by your dimmers so that it can be carried out during an intermission if necessary.

SWITCHING MODULES AND TRIMMING

Unless you have electronics experience, the only other procedure you may periodically carry out on your dimmers is trimming them. Many dimmer modules allow the adjustment of the minimum level and maximum level achieved throughout the range of the dimmer. If the minimum level is too high, the dimmer will continue to put out some level of voltage to the fixtures, causing them to glow or "ghost" when the control board is at zero. If it is too low, the fixtures may seem to pop on or off at some level on the control board's scale instead of giving a gradual fade. Some manufacturers include the procedure for setting the trim on dimmers in their manuals. It usually can be carried out with a standard small blade screwdriver, a test load (a light of at least 100 watts plugged into the dimmer output), and a "true RMS" volt meter. If you do not have access to a "true RMS" volt meter, you will have to determine how your meter reacts to the voltage waveform found at the output of your particular dimmers. False readings can be seen if the meter and waveform are not compatible.

For adjusting the minimum trim, the test load is plugged into the dimmer and the lower trim adjusted to where the light just goes off at a setting of zero on the control board. After adjusting the minimum trim, the maximum trim must always be checked. This is done by setting the control fader to a reading of 10 and measuring the output at the dimmer. The maximum trim should be adjusted until the reading is 120V RMS. Procedures vary from manufacturer to manufacturer. Consult your manual or contact the dimmer manufacturer for the proper procedure to follow.

TIE-INS

Dimmer packs can usually be set up for either single phase three-wire or three phase four-wire electrical systems. This can often be changed by switching one or two wires inside the pack. This procedure should be pointed out in the literature supplied with the pack, or you could ask the manufacturer for a copy of the procedure. This way the pack could be changed to fit the house system, when needed. If a pack is set up for one configuration and tied into another the pack can be seriously damaged, so be careful. Before doing anything with a system be sure you know what you are dealing with. There are many different possible set-ups, each of which can need a different setup with each dimmer manufacturer type or design. One supply configuration that can prove particularly problematic is what is referred to as a *delta system*. This is a three phase four-wire system, but the middle leg (phase B) is "high," reading 208V to neutral instead of the more common 120V from each leg to neutral, and only the other two legs (phases A and C) read 120V between the leg and neutral.

If you ever come across this system, be sure you speak to the dimmer manufacturer for the proper means of tying into it. Most often it must be treated as a single phase three-wire system, using only the A and C legs to tie n the dimmers. In the chapter on electricity it is noted that tie-ins can be *very dangerous* if you are not familiar with what you are doing. A mistake can destroy your equipment, the facility, or somebody's life. Be sure whoever is tying your system into the house electrical system knows exactly what he or she is doing. There are different methods used to tie dimmers into a power distribution system. Most often pigtails are used with bare ends on one end and a connector of some design (camloc, union, etc.) on the other. With power to the disconnect off, the pigtails are tied into the lugs in the power disconnect of the building: green to ground, white to neutral, and blue, red and black to the hot lugs on a three phase four-wire system. One of the hot legs is omitted in a single phase three-wire system, otherwise the color coding remains the same. Using the connectors on the pigtails, power feed cables are then either run directly to the dimmer packs or to a power distribution box which is used to power several dimmer packs.

POWER DISTRIBUTION BOXES

Power distribution boxes, referred to as "PD" boxes, consist of input connectors for tying into the building distribution system, over-current protection devices of some form, power indicators, and output connectors to feed power to the dimmer packs being supplied by the PD box. You must try to *balance the load* on a distribution system by tying similar capacities of dimmers across all the available hot legs.

REPATCHING

One way to work your dimmers (probably your largest lighting investment) as far as possible is to repatch or replug during the show. If a fixture is only used in a particular segment of a show and another during a different segment, you can run a jumper to a convenient spot to replug them during the show and use only one dimmer for both (or several) fixtures.

There is a device made to facilitate this called an AB switch box (you can also make one easily). An AB switch box allows you to switch the fixtures controlled by a dimmer by merely throwing a switch. These boxes are also available with a remote box so that you can switch back and forth during the show from the control board. (Do not switch while fixtures are on.) They are generally a fraction of the cost of a bank of dimmers and effectively double a bank of dimmers' capacity. Combine one of these with some replugging

and regelling between acts or sets, and you can have an extremely varied show for a lower investment.

QUALITY AND VALUE

As you look into buying a system be sure you are getting your money's worth. A rock bottom price tag can indicate a lesser value, while the highest price tag doesn't have to mean the highest quality or best value. At times corners are cut such as using insufficient filtering (have you ever heard that awful hum in the amps of a band?) or underrated components to keep costs down. Get the spec sheets and compare. Call the various manufacturers. You are spending good money, so take the time to make sure you are making an investment, not just getting the cheapest system. Ask for a listing of places using the equipment you are interested in and give them a call. Find out if they are happy with the equipment. A minor savings up-front could cost you your show somewhere down the road.

PART III
Lighting the Show

Paperwork

Whenever you create a lighting design you should take the time to generate at least five pieces of paperwork: a light plot, an elevation view, a hookup, a magic sheet, and cue sheets. It is also necessary to make a bill of materials, but this is often done by the electrician in charge of preparation (if this doesn't happen to be you).

Each of these documents will help get the show up and running with the least worry or confusion. They also allow you to create and improvise quickly, particularly in the event of a problem requiring you to trouble-shoot on the run.

LIGHT PLOT

The light plot is a schematic of the lighting fixture layout. It is a plan view or floor plan of the hardware used to execute your design. It is the stage with the electrics and lighting fixtures viewed from above as if the theater ceiling had been removed and you were looking down at the stage from the sky. It shows the distances stage left to stage right as well as upstage and downstage.

Symbols

Each fixture type has a unique symbol on the plot, which should be shown on a key along with the scale of the plot. Each electric is also indicated on the plot, often with the trim height indicated in a circled dimension. The symbol for each fixture in a design is placed on the plot as close to where it is to be hung on stage as possible. This way an electrician can use a scale rule to measure approximately where the instrument is to hang. On or near each symbol the focus area, color, circuit number, dimmer number, and fixture number are given. If there is room, the control channel number may also appear.

The USITT (United States Institute for Theatre Technology) has established standard symbols for the most common fixture types, though any symbol may be used as long as it is explained in the key. The fixture symbols are usually aimed in the general direction in which they are to be focused. Some designers prefer the appearance of having all the fixtures on a plot pointing in the same direction. The plot should be as clear, neat, and informative as possible. It will be a map for setups and a guide for troubleshooting.

Make several copies and NEVER work with your original unless you so enjoy doing a plot that you are looking for an excuse to do it over. The various focus areas should be lightly indicated in as clear and uncluttered a fashion as you can devise. Letters are often used. Some designers like to draw the outlines of the settings lightly onto their plot for reference. Others prefer not to clutter the plot any more than necessary, so they lay the page on which they are drawing the plot over a copy of the set floor plan, or they use a computer to draw the settings on different "layers" that can be turned on and off when needed, to position the electrics better. This method allows the setting page to be changed for different scenes to keep a clearer view of what is happening than when all the major components are sketched in one plot.

Scale

Your light plot should be drawn to some scale that will allow the position of the lighting fixtures on the stage to be measured off the plot. Plots are most often drawn in ⅛", ¼", or ½" = 1'-0" scale. This means if you are using ¼" = 1'-0" scale (also called ¼" scale) every ¼" on your plot represents 1'-0" on the actual stage. Many designers prefer to use the smallest scale that allows a clear and legible plot to be rendered without becoming too cumbersome.

Paper

Light plots are most often drawn on vellum, or drafting paper. This is a translucent paper that allows the creation of copies using a blueprint machine. It is similar to tracing paper only of heavier stock. If you do not have ready access to a machine for blueprint making, you should be able to find a local business offering the

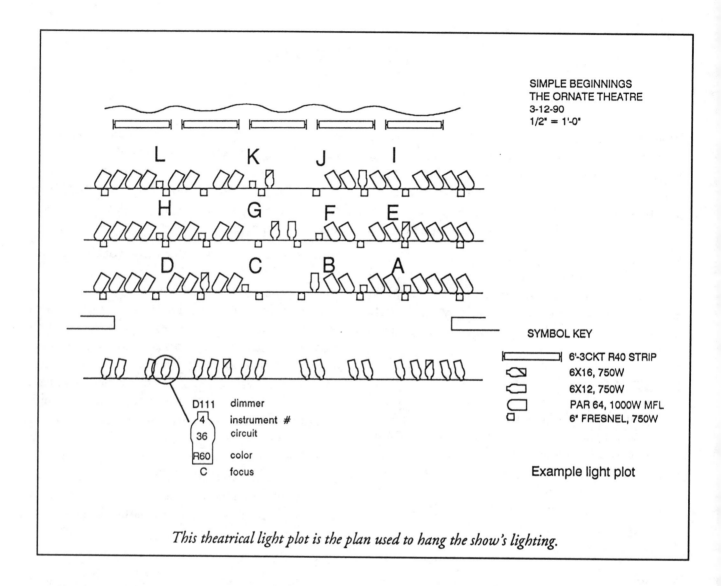

SIMPLE BEGINNINGS
THE ORNATE THEATRE
3-12-90
1/2" = 1'-0"

SYMBOL KEY

▭	6'-3CKT R40 STRIP
◁	6X16, 750W
◁	6X12, 750W
⬭	PAR 64, 1000W MFL
◻	6" FRESNEL, 750W

Example light plot

D111 — dimmer
4 — instrument #
36 — circuit
R60 — color
C — focus

This theatrical light plot is the plan used to hang the show's lighting.

service of producing blueprints from your originals. Such services are usually listed in the yellow pages under either blueprint services or drafting supplies. The process isn't very expensive, and is usually priced by the square foot of drawing.

The different sizes of vellum used for light plots include "A" — 8½" x 11" (used mostly for ⅛" = 1'-0" plots), "B" — 11" x 17" (used for ⅛" and ¼" scales), "C" — 17" x 22" (used mostly for ¼" scale), "D" — 22" x 34" (used mostly for ½" scale), and "E" — 34" x 44" (used almost exclusively for ½" scale). "C" and "D" are the most commonly used sizes.

Drafting

The manual drafting needed to create a quality light plot is fairly easy, not requiring most of the more

expensive equipment used for higher accuracy drawings used in manufacturing.

You should use a drawing board of ample size to fit the size drawing of your choice with some room to spare, and should have the corners perfectly square (90° to next side). You will need a squaring device for drawing horizontal lines — either a T-square (the most basic style), a square rule (straightedge on cable track), or a drafting machine (two straight edges 90° apart, mounted on a pivot with protractor, all mounted on a retractable arm). A 45°/45° and a 30°/60° triangle are needed for vertical lines and lines at angles, along with a protractor for measuring angles, unless you have a drafting machine, which takes care of all these functions. You will also need a scale rule. An architect's rule — a three-sided rule with an assortment of

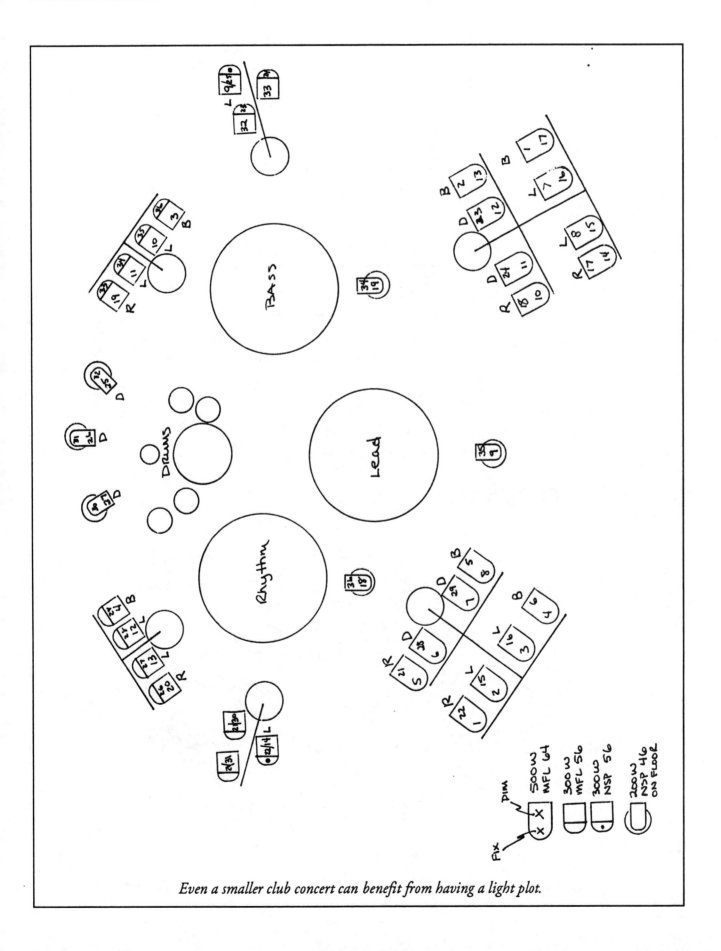

Even a smaller club concert can benefit from having a light plot.

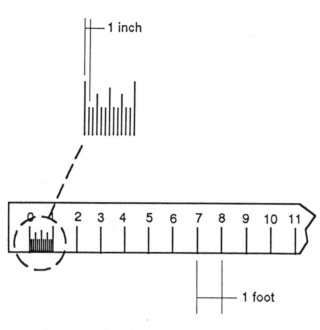

1/4" = 1'-0" scale

The scale rule used by architects allows convenient scale drawing for light plots.

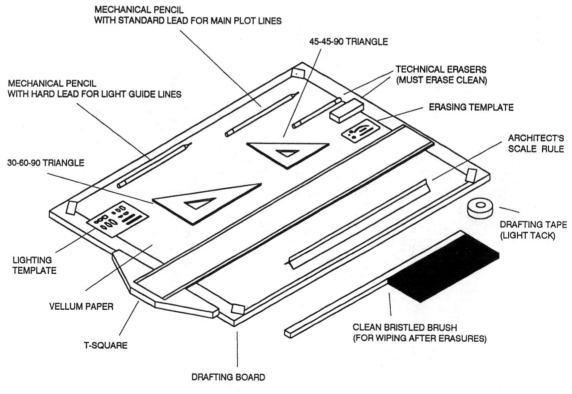

Only the most basic drafting tools are required to create a "professional" light plot.

different scales laid out on it, including ⅛", ¼", and ½" scales — is the most commonly used kind of scale rule. Good quality pencils or lead holders and lead, a good pencil or lead sharpener, and high quality erasers are essential. Inking a plot is unnecessary. Make the pencil lines dark enough to reproduce well but not too dark so they can be easily erased should the need arise. An erasing template can be extremely useful for keeping your plot clean when changes occur. A lighting template to speed the use of standard lighting symbols is a good tool to have. The lighting template produces a clearer plot that tends to eliminate many mistakes made by others when reading the plot. It also helps to have a compass for drawing circles of various diameters as well as a circle template for your most common sizes.

There are a number of good books available about basic drafting techniques. Any one of them presents ample information on the use of the equipment to allow you to produce high quality plots. All the drafting supplies required can be found in almost any art or drafting supply store, or by mail order. Sources for lighting templates are advertised in theatrical trade magazines. Refer to this book's Appendix containing useful addresses for how to contact some magazines, stores, and a manufacturer of lighting templates.

Be sure to have decent lighting when working at your drawing board. If you don't, eye fatigue and strain can slow things down quickly.

Computer-Aided Drafting

Computer-aided drafting (CAD) programs can be very useful for drawing the light plot. With most programs, the lighting symbols are only drawn once. They can be quickly duplicated, or inserted, wherever needed. Some of the more sophisticated programs also allow the symbols to have information attached to them so that after the plot is complete a bill of materials and a hookup can be generated from the plot automatically. Several programs have been written specifically for stage lighting and include the ability to generate hookups and circuit charts automatically, as well as pick fixtures by beam characteristics required.

Though the computer is hard to compete with when it comes to organizing your information into different lists and reports, such as the bill of materials, hookup, and patch chart, there are some drawbacks to using a computer to generate plots. One large drawback is the amount of money that must be invested to be able to generate a light plot of even equal quality to the plot generated by hand. A large capacity fast computer is needed, often with special hardware to suit the CAD program chosen. The monitor and video card must be able to produce very high quality graphics, and you must have some kind of output device to plot out the finished product, not a dot matrix printer. In addition, there is a high learning curve as well as the task of creating the symbols before creating the first plot. There may be libraries of stage lighting symbols available for some of the CAD systems in use. You should find out what is available before buying into a system.

Using a computer may also necessitate drawing the settings in before starting your plot. This step is not necessary when manually drafting the plot because you can draw your plot in the same scale as the set floor plan and lay your plot over a copy of the set, or quickly trace parts of the setting onto it if you prefer. The computer system needed for manipulating lists and reports is relatively inexpensive, costing the same as a professional quality typewriter. A quality dot matrix printer and a basic monochrome monitor are all that are needed. The equipment used to generate quality plots from a CAD system costs as much as a new car, or more. That kind of investment could take a long time to pay for itself. The cost is especially difficult to justify in light of the fact that, using templates, a quality hand-drawn plot can often be generated as fast if not faster than a computer-generated one. Also changes that occur on light plots are most often not of the nature that make it easier to do in CAD than by hand. A computer CAD system is not as portable as manual drafting, something that should be considered if you design lights for performances that require you to travel.

ELEVATION VIEW

An elevation view is a side view of the stage, usually from stage right looking on stage. At this angle, downstage and the audience would be to the right of the

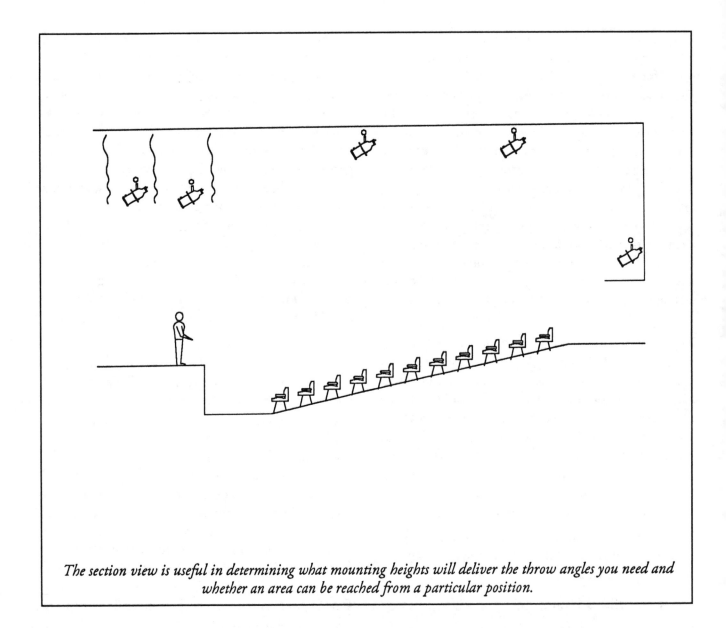

The section view is useful in determining what mounting heights will deliver the throw angles you need and whether an area can be reached from a particular position.

drawing and upstage to the left. The elevation shows the distances upstage and downstage as well as the vertical distances.

This drawing should be made to scale so that you can directly measure angles off it. Even though your linear measurements are scaled down, your angles will be the same. An elevation can be a neatly drafted formal drawing that is later given to the electricians to aid in hanging the show, or it can be a rough sketch drawn to scale for your own use. There are lighting templates available showing the fixtures from the side for quick elevation views. If the electricians are not given an elevation view you will need to indicate the trim heights of electrics on the light plot. In either case, the elevation helps determine how far up or downstage the fixtures should be from their subjects, as well as how high from the stage floor they should be to give the proper aim angle.

It is common to sketch a performer onto the stage to better illustrate what is happening. The figure should be between five feet four inches and six feet tall. If you are lighting a show with much shorter or taller performers, you should include their heights on the drawing to make sure they are covered.

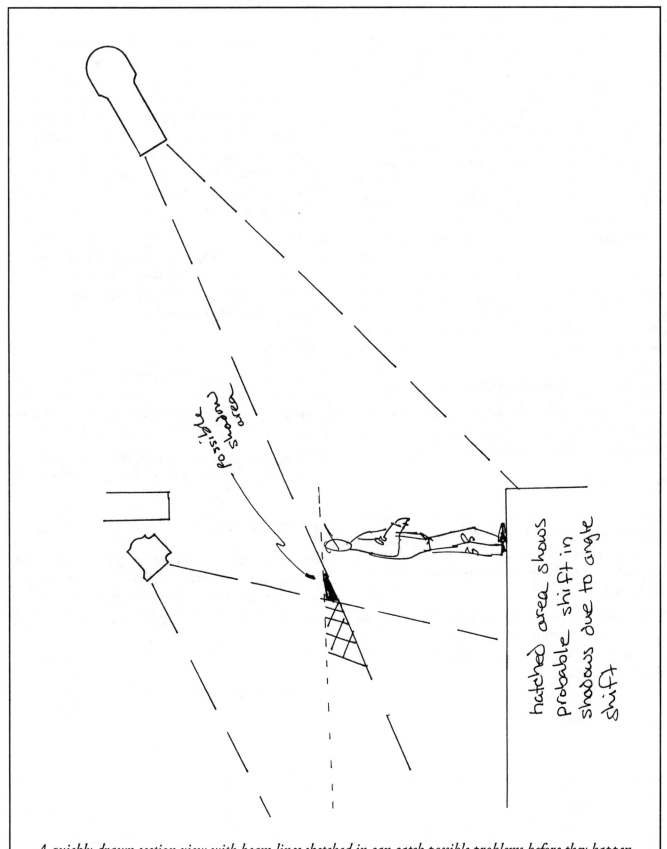

A quickly drawn section view with beam lines sketched in can catch possible problems before they happen.

If an elevation view is sketched viewing it at a right angle to the light plot line from fixture to subject, throw distances can be directly read off the elevation using a scale rule lined up from the fixture to the subject being lit. You can also lightly sketch in the beam spread of a fixture at its beam angle to see how it will cover the area. This is very important since all the calculations given are to determine the beam diameters of fixtures thrown against a surface perpendicular to the fixture. This is not the actual case on the stage. The light is being cast at a different angle to the floor as well as to a performer on the stage. You are actually using what is called a conic section of light, or an ellipse. There are engineering formulas for determining what the actual conic sections are, but it is much easier just to see what is happening in an elevation view. More area will be covered in line with a beam of light than across the beam. This is the case for the area covered parallel to the stage and for the area parallel to a performer standing on the stage, when the beam shines down 45° off horizontal.

The elevation is a very valuable tool that is too often skipped when laying out a show. Many problems may be avoided if one is properly laid out.

HOOKUP

The hookup is a couple of listings, one that shows what circuits are in which dimmers and one that shows what dimmers are in which control channels (not necessary if the channels and dimmer numbers are the same).

The hookup can save a great deal of time during setup and also speeds up troubleshooting the system. Take the time to list every thing in both directions (i.e., circuit-dimmer and dimmer-circuit).

MAGIC SHEET

The magic sheet is a group of small sketches — rough tiny plots — one for each control channel. Each sketch has the control channel number, general description (such as cool side wash SL, purple back wash ...) and a sketch of the outline of the stage with arrows representing each fixture on the channel pointing to where it is focused from approximately where it hangs. Each arrow should have the circuit (and dimmer if different from control channel) that it is hooked into and possibly the color.

The magic sheet is gold when trying to design on the fly or when something isn't working and you have to supplement fast. Don't get too involved, keep them simple. Get as many on one page as possible with the information still easily readable.

CUE SHEET

A cue sheet is a listing of the levels of each channel of a scene for each different cue. Any layout can be used as long as it is possible to read it quickly since preparing for a cue or presetting a scene must be done fast.

Information such as channel settings, cue entrance speeds, cue exit speeds, and notes on when the cue is to occur should appear on the cue sheet.

BILL OF MATERIALS

The bill of materials lists everything you need for the plot to be executed: dimmers, fixtures with lamps, gel cuts, cable runs, etc. The section on pre-production details more about what should appear on a bill of materials.

HOOK-UP   Page 1 of 2

circuit	dimmer	circuit	dimmer
1	3	31	34
2	6	32	35
3	9	33	36
4	24	34	18
5	6	35	13
6	14	36	17
7	30	37	3
8	28	38	19
9	28	39	22
10	23	40	22
11	4	41	12
12	18	42	7
13	12	43	9
14	8	44	13
15	5	45	16
16	31	46	5
17	33	47	34
18	27	48	35
19	7	49	36
20	12	50	--
21	19	51	1
22	21	52	15
23	10	53	28
24	11	54	26
25	18	55	11
26	2	56	5
27	22	57	34
28	16	58	35
29	1	59	36
30	8	60	15

The hookup (circuit/dimmer) will save time when plugging, or patching, the show.

Dimmer / Circuit
   Hook-up

Dimmer	Circuits	Dimmer	Circuits
1 —	29, 51	21 -	22
2 —	26	22 -	27, 39, 40
3 —	1, 37	23 -	10
4 -	11	24 -	4
5 -	46, 56, 15	25 -	NOT USED
6 -	2, 5	26 -	54
7 -	42, 19	27 -	18
8 -	30, 14	28 -	8, 9, 53
9 -	3, 43	29 -	NOT USED
10 -	23	30 -	7
11 -	24, 55	31 -	16
12 -	13, 20, 41	32 -	~~17~~ not used
13 -	35, 44	33 -	17
14 -	6	34 -	31, 47, 57
15 -	52, 60	35 -	32, 58, 48
16 -	28, 45	36 -	33, 49, 59
17 -	36		
18 -	12, 25, 34		
19 -	21, 38		
20 -	OUT OF SERVICE		

The hookup reversed (dimmer/circuit) will save time when something is not working or substitutions need to be made.

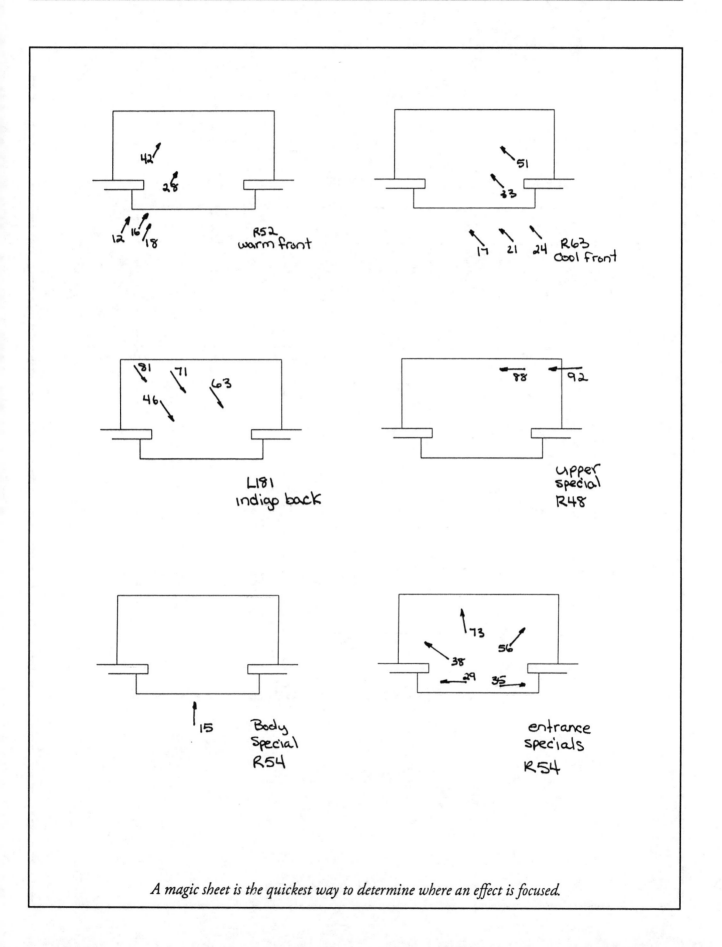

A magic sheet is the quickest way to determine where an effect is focused.

CUE # ___63___   ACT/SCENE ___I·5___

1	2	3	4	5	6
6	6	3	8	7	8

7	8	9	10	11	12
Ø	2	2	4	8	9

13	14	15	16	17	18
7	7	Ø	Ø	10	9

Description: 15 count
on entrance of sister.

The cue sheet should be clean and easy to read.

Page 5

50) $\underline{1^{10} \; 2^8 \; 4^6 \; 5^6 \; 7^8 \; 9^6 \; 10^{10} \; 11^{10} \; 12^3 \; 15^5 \; 16^5 \; 17^6}$

51) $1\downarrow_4 \; 6\uparrow^6 \; 8\uparrow^6$

52) $7\downarrow_5 \; 8\downarrow_4 \; 12\uparrow^7$

53) $18\uparrow^4$

54) $\underline{4^6 \; 7^5 \; 8^4 \; 9^5 \; 11^3 \; 15^3 \; 16^3 \; 17^4 \; 18^2}$

55) $10\uparrow^6$

56) $11\uparrow^6 \; 12\uparrow^6 \; 17\downarrow_0$

   replug 17

57) $9\downarrow_0 \; 12\downarrow_4 \; 14\uparrow^3$

58) $17\uparrow^5$

   replug 9

59) $9\uparrow^6$ .rest of stage $\downarrow_0$ <u>slow</u>

Intermission

   repeat preshow

$\underline{1^3 \; 6^2 \; 8^2 \; 11^4 \; 14^6 \; 17^3 \; 18^2}$

replug 9 & 17

A compact form of cue sheet that works best for preset boards with twenty-four channels or less.
New presets are underlined; internal changes are indicated with arrows.

Bill of Materials - Lighting
Page 1 of 3

Fixtures

All fixtures to be equipped with 20A-M2P&G plug, colorframe, C clamp, and safety cable.

Ellipsoidals -

6x9 - 500W..EHD..................	18
6x9 - 750W..EHG..................	11
6x12- 500W..EHD..................	8
6x12- 750W..EHG..................	17
6x16- 750W..EHG..................	22
6x16- 1000W.FEL..................	9

Fresnels -

6" - 750W...BTN..................	14
8" - 1000W..BVT..................	11
8" - 1500W..CWZ..................	3

PARS -

64 - 500W..MFL..................	19
64 - 1000W.MFL.FFR..............	11
64 - 1000W.NSP.FFP..............	12
46 - 300W..NSP..................	9

FLOODS -

Mini-Flood - 500W.FDN............	16

STRIPS/CYCS -

6' Mini-Strip 50W EXZ.............	6
6' Mini-Strip 50W EXT.............	6
6' R40, 3ckt.150W.R/FL............	4

Accessories

6" Pattern holders................	11
7-1/2" Donut......................	11
Patterns.........................see separate list	
6" 8-way barn door................	9
8" 8-way barn door................	6
Piggy-back Mini-Strip trunion......6pr	
Single side arm w/ tee............	14

A bill of materials compiles everything needed to mount the show's lighting.

Troubleshooting Your System

No matter how hard we try, things go wrong. In fact, it sometimes seems that the harder we try, the more that goes wrong. At some point you will be faced with something that does not work, and you will have very little time to fix it. If you approach the situation calmly and logically, you can get everything up and running in time. There is an easy approach to any troubleshooting job whether you are fixing a lighting system, sound system, TV, stereo, whatever. The success of the method depends on your understanding what each stage (in a lighting system the stages would be fixture, circuit, dimmer, control channel ... a sound system would have speaker, amplifier, mixing console, microphone ...) does for the entire system.

DETERMINING CAUSE AND EFFECT

It is generally not important to know *how* as long as you know *what*. When you know what each stage does you can use cause and effect to determine quickly where a problem can originate. First, try to look at the problem as an effect. This can take some of the pressure off. How would you *create* this effect (problem)? You look at the symptoms and guess which stage would do that. You then go to the "last" stage that could be in question and start testing back to front (in a lighting system this would be from the fixture to the control board, in a radio it would be speaker to antenna) to see where things STOP going wrong. You have then found where the problem lies.

Looking at the most common example — a fixture doesn't light — where could this problem originate? The last stage that could be at fault would actually be the last stage, the fixture itself. Go to the fixture, unplug it, and check to see if there is power at the outlet the fixture was plugged into. If there is, check the fixture with an ohm meter or continuity tester to see if there is a complete circuit. If there is not, either the fixture wiring or the lamp is at fault. If the lamp checks out okay with an ohm meter, then the fixture wiring must be the source of the problem. Check the connector first, since a problem there is much more common than a problem with the actual fixture wiring. If there is no power at the fixture, the next thing to check is whether there is power at the other end of the circuit or at the dimmer output. Keep tracing back toward the control board in this fashion until things test out correctly. The last stage that checks out in error is the source of the problem. Had all the fixtures on one dimmer not worked, you would start at the dimmer output and test back from there.

Always make sure there is no power on before opening any piece of equipment. Don't trust a switch; disconnect when possible, then test it.

TOOLS

It is very easy to troubleshoot any system as long as you *think*. You should also make things easier for yourself by having the proper tools on hand for emergencies. Aside from the usual fuses, spare cables, and lamps you should carry at least the following tools in your supply box:

- gloves (for heat)
- flashlight
- portable multimeter with AC volts (200V range), DC volts (12V range), ohms (resistance), and possibly an audible continuity test. Radio Shack has some very reliable, affordable meters available.
- medium and small standard screwdrivers
- #1 and #2 Phillips screwdrivers
- knife (a sharp one)
- wire stripper
- lineman's pliers (flat-nosed pliers with side wire cutter)
- 8-inch adjustable wrench
- ¼-inch nut driver
- teaspoon (Nothing else gets a broken lamp out of a medium or mogul prefocus socket better. Just be sure to unplug the fixture before you try to use it. Jam it in and turn it counterclockwise; it works every time.)

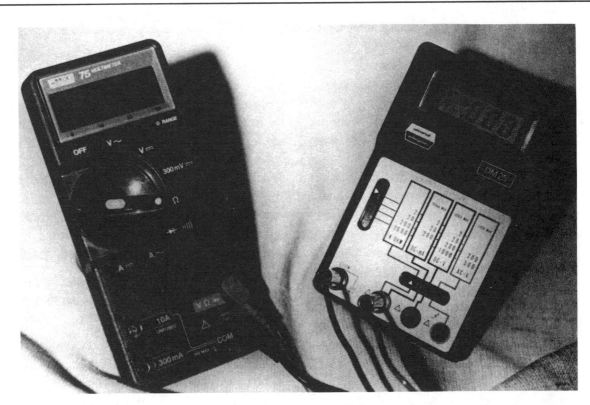

Continuity test — good.

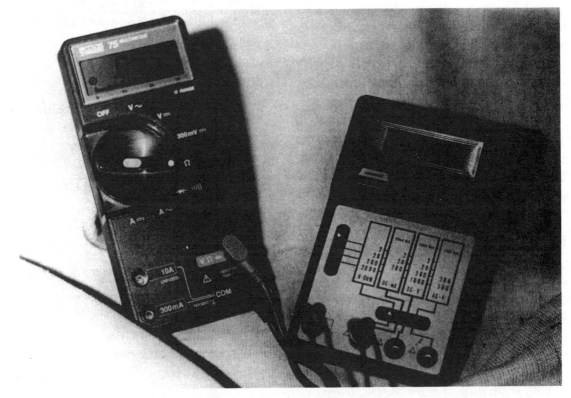

Continuity test — no good (note that some digital meters show OL and some 1).

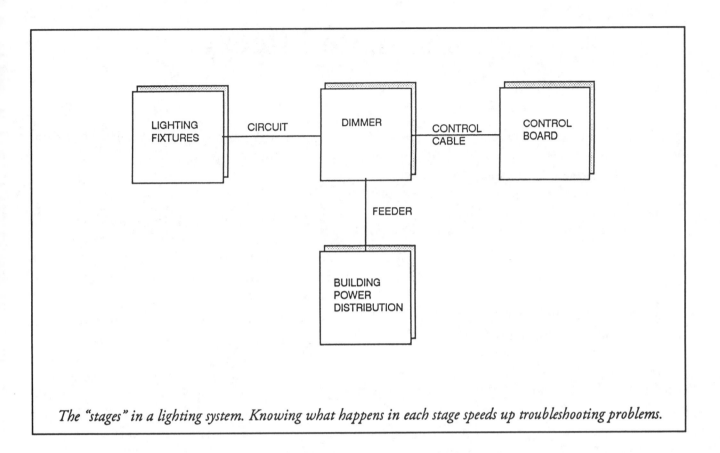

The "stages" in a lighting system. Knowing what happens in each stage speeds up troubleshooting problems.

These tools represent a modest investment and are completely necessary to carry out your job.

WHEN YOU CAN'T FIX IT IN TIME

The last thing you should remember is that sometimes things just can't be fixed in time. You have to be able to recognize when you won't be able to fix it and give yourself the time required to go to plan B (which may not exist until you need it) and get creative.

Homemade Effects

There are several popular effects you can create that can add to the visual effectiveness of a design. In this chapter we will discuss how some of these effects can be created. They include a light box or shadow box, a moon/sun box, a chaser strip, lightning, sunlight, and a unique effect used to set up a special stage for both puppetry and mime.

LIGHT BOX

A light box, or shadow box, is more a part of the set than of the lighting design, but it falls under the responsibility of the electrician or lighting designer at many theaters. There are a number of ways to build light boxes. The following description is just one suggestion.

For the light source, you can use either standard A-type lamps or fluorescent lamps. If you intend to dim the box you should use A lamps. The actual effect is that of a backlit painting or silhouette. First, you build a box 6 to 8 inches deep and 6 inches larger in both width and height than the painting or silhouette being backlit. The painting should be dye-painted cloth, glass, or plastic. The inside sides and back of the box should be painted a very matte white.

The lamps are placed around the inside perimeter of the box and masked so that they do not shine directly on the painting or silhouette. If A-type lamps are used, they can be placed on 4- to 6-inch centers, and fluorescent lamps should run along the sides. In this way the painting is only lit by the indirect light reflecting off the matte white backing, giving a very even illumination across the painting. Generally, you should not use over 60 watt A lamps, or 40 watt fluorescent lamps in the box.

It may be necessary to vent the sides and top of the box to prevent too much heat from building up. When light boxes are built into a set, they can be effectively masked so that they are not revealed until they are actually lit, creating a very dramatic effect. One method is to have a dark scrim mounted several inches in front of the painting.

MOON BOX OR SUN BOX

The moon box or sun box is very similar to the light box in construction. The only difference is that instead of having a painting mounted to the front, a round opening (or crescent if a partial moon is needed) is cut into the front.

This box is almost always made using incandescent lamps, generally A-type. It is important that the lamps are masked so that they do not directly shine out of the opening in the box. The box is hung a couple of inches upstage of a scrim. When the box is lit a very effective moon or sun is projected onto the scrim. If the box is mounted onto a pulley system, different positions may be used during a performance.

CHASER STRIPS

You can easily construct your own chaser strips for lining runways, set pieces, or whatever other use you may have for them. A chaser strip is simply a multiple circuit strip (even a regular striplight or borderlight can be used) with each circuit turned on and off in sequence.

You can buy a chaser controller from a lighting control manufacturer or electronic effect shop, and set the strip up using a programmable chase feature on your control board. Or if you have electronics experience, you can wire your own chasing control box. A chasing strip can be made by mounting a line of sockets onto a board or base of some design. Be sure the base will not be able either to short out the circuit or to become overheated and burn. The sockets of a circuit are then wired in parallel to each other as in a borderlight, skipping the sockets of the other circuits. One end of the circuit should start with a cable terminated with some kind of plug, then each conductor of the cable (black — hot and white — neutral, not green —

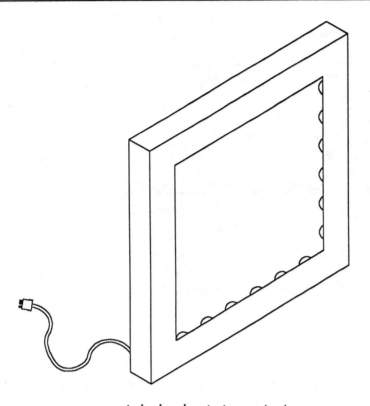

A shadow box in isometric view.

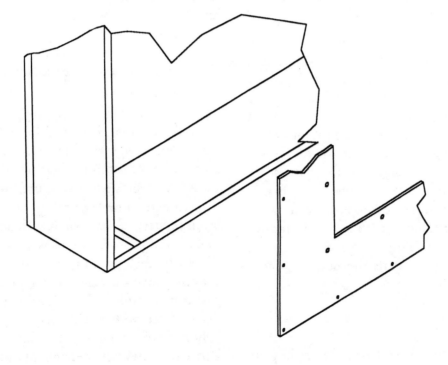

An exploded view of the shadow box construction. Wood construction is most often used.

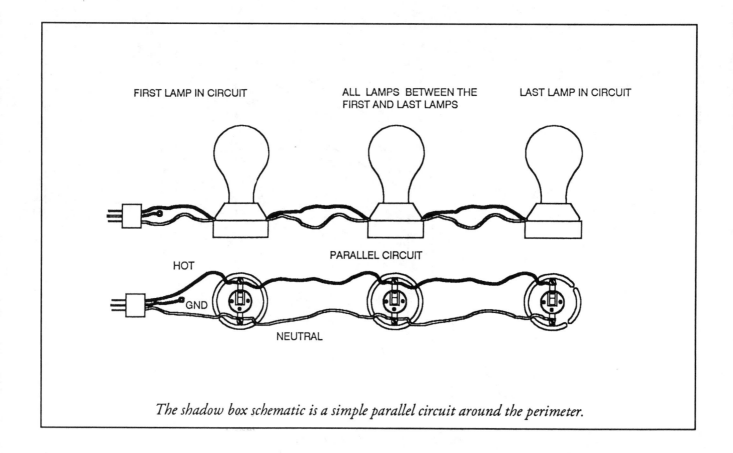

FIRST LAMP IN CIRCUIT

ALL LAMPS BETWEEN THE
FIRST AND LAST LAMPS

LAST LAMP IN CIRCUIT

PARALLEL CIRCUIT

HOT

GND

NEUTRAL

The shadow box schematic is a simple parallel circuit around the perimeter.

ground) is attached to the corresponding terminal of each socket of the circuit.

Any style socket will do as long as it fits the lamps you intend to use. You can wire as many circuits into a strip as you wish. The most common chasing strips have three or four circuits. You should end up with the same number of plugs at one end as you have circuits in the strip. These plugs are then plugged into whatever device will power the circuits when they are needed. The lamps commonly used for chaser strips are small clear, white, or colored globe lamps, candle lamps, or sign lamps. These lamps are commonly available with either edium screw, intermediate screw, or candelabra bases. With any screw-shell type socket, the screw-shell is attached to the neutral (white) conductor.

STROBE LIGHTS

Strobe lights used to cover a large area brightly are quite expensive. Most rental houses have them available. If, however, you find this is not a viable option,

it is possible to simulate the effect using a small motor and making a bracket to mount it in front of one of your lights and a wheel similar to that found on a colorwheel, only with narrow cutouts. A variable speed motor, such as those used on ceiling fans, works best.

This piece of equipment is similar to the old-fashioned *lobster scope*. It is ideal for old-time movie effects. Many people agree that it is more effective than a strobe light for this application. You should know the RPM (revolutions per minute) rating of the motor to help determine how to lay out the front wheel layout; otherwise, you will have to use trial and error to find the proper layout. You can figure out the RPM's by making a mark on the center stem and counting how many times the stem turns per minute. To create a strobe effect with the unit, you need to make a wheel with cutout openings spaced so that the lighting fixture it mounts onto shines through them at a pace of somewhere between one and twenty times per second, depending on how fast a strobe effect you desire. It is best to use a faster motor to do this so that the openings can be spaced far enough apart on the wheel to allow the light to be completely cut off between flashes, without any part of an opening overlapping the light before the previous one has passed.

Be sure the entire rig is safely secured so that it does not eventually vibrate loose and fall on someone's head. You should have separate power feeds to the motor and the light fixture. You do not want to try dimming a motor on a standard theatrical dimmer. If you do not want the effect of the slow start building to full speed, you must turn the motor on shortly before the light to give it time to reach full speed first.

LIGHTNING

One of the most common special effects is the creation of lightning. There are possibly as many different methods used to create lightning as there are lighting designers. Effects range from flashing, or bumping, the area lighting up to full momentarily to using various forms of pyrotechnics. If you are going to use some form of quickly flashing several lights to full for a second or two, be sure to experiment with the fixtures you intend to use. Some lamps' filaments are so large and slow to respond that their burn-down rate is too slow for effective lighting effects. PAR lamps often fall into this category. Most high wattage incandescent lamps have this problem. One way to get around this is to use lower voltage lamps. Most low voltage lamps used in stage lighting, such as MR-16 lamps in strips, ACL lamps in PAR's, and pinspot lamps in PAR rainlights, respond fairly quickly to control and burn down quite rapidly to give a fast on and off cycle.

The quick flashing of various instruments not containing any color gel is probably the most convenient as well as effective method available to create lightning. It is further enhanced if the control board operator can convey the random pulsing look most commonly seen during an electrical storm. This random quality of lightning can be further enhanced if your control board has a chase program feature available. It must be carefully planned to work properly. The chase is programmed to sequence between a number

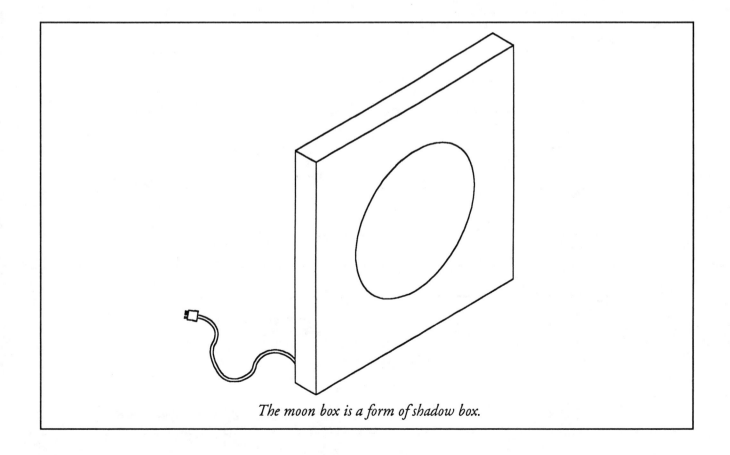

The moon box is a form of shadow box.

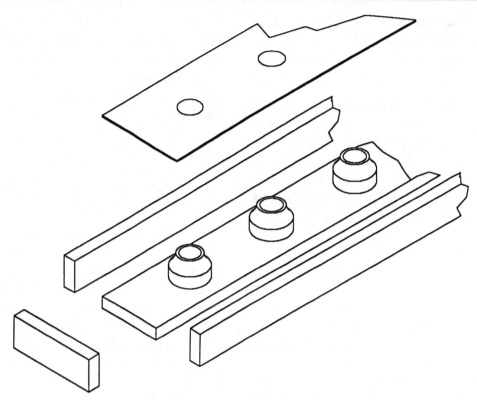

A chaser strip can be constructed relatively easily.

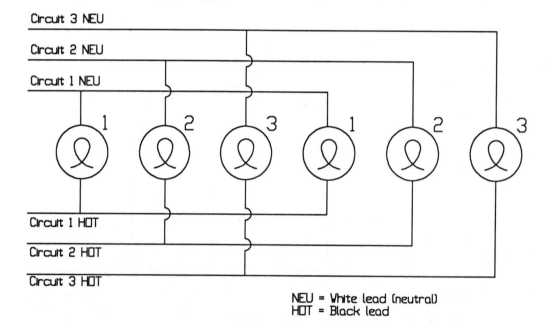

Circuit 3 NEU

Circuit 2 NEU

Circuit 1 NEU

1   2   3   1   2   3

Circuit 1 HOT

Circuit 2 HOT

Circuit 3 HOT

NEU = White lead (neutral)
HOT = Black lead

3 CIRCUIT CHASER

The chaser strip schematic consists of several parallel circuits alternating with each other.

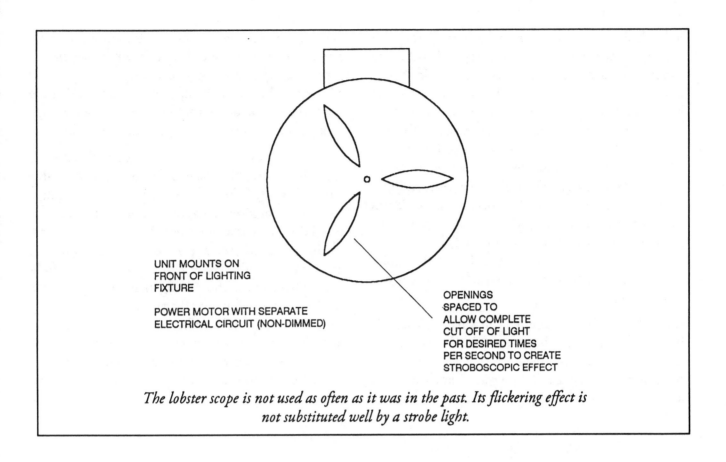

UNIT MOUNTS ON
FRONT OF LIGHTING
FIXTURE

POWER MOTOR WITH SEPARATE
ELECTRICAL CIRCUIT (NON-DIMMED)

OPENINGS
SPACED TO
ALLOW COMPLETE
CUT OFF OF LIGHT
FOR DESIRED TIMES
PER SECOND TO CREATE
STROBOSCOPIC EFFECT

The lobster scope is not used as often as it was in the past. Its flickering effect is not substituted well by a strobe light.

of fixtures, all without gel, laid out around the stage in what should appear to be no real pattern, making the light scatter all around the stage. It should not be allowed to run through more than one cycle so it will seem very haphazard.

Another very effective lightning effect simulating very close lightning strikes can be created using the small flashbulbs available with medium screw bases. This method can become rather expensive if a large number of lightning flashes are needed and you are going to do a number of performances. The method is carried out two different ways, depending on the control system you have available. You should also try the method out before buying too many bulbs, since some over-current protection devices are too sensitive and will trip when a flash bulb is set off on their circuit.

The method requires a few different circuits for the bulbs. If you have a board with a programmable chase, the same effect is done as described above except the fixtures are equipped with the flashbulbs. If more than one lightning flash is needed, programs for different circuits are required.

Another method is to run a number of non-dim circuits around the stage with a bank of toggle switches to control them. The lightning is set off by quickly throwing the switches in whatever sequence you decide upon. It is important to have the fixtures with the flash bulbs out of the line of sight of the audience so that just the flash of light is seen. Sometimes several bulbs on separate circuits are built into a large light box as described above and this is used as sort of a lightning projector.

SUNLIGHT

Sunlight is another effect commonly required on stage. To simulate sunlight effectively, either as a full stage wash or a beam through an open window, you must understand a couple of basic facts about real sunlight. These are that sunlight is light that travels in parallel beams, and it only throws one shadow. If an individual shaft of light is to be created to shine through something, such as a window, it is best to choose an instrument that uses a parabolic-shaped reflector. Parabolic reflectors throw light in parallel beams. PAR lamps have parabolic reflectors but the actual beam of light is changed somewhat by the lens built into the lamp. They are often used for sunlight effects anyway. The instrument known as the beam projector is used almost exclusively to create sunlight effects. It contains a parabolic reflector with no lenses to alter the shaft of light produced. Beam projectors are becoming less common because they have limited use compared to most fixtures and tend to require more maintenance and do not perform well if not properly set up.

If a wash of sunlight is required you will need to decide if a single fixture covering the area is adequate or if a number of fixtures are required. The advantage of a single fixture is that it will throw only one shadow. As long as it is bright enough to wash out the shadows created by the other fixtures used for toning and supporting the scene, the feeling of a sunny day will be supported. If possible, try to have the fixture as far away from the subject being lit as you can, so that the shadow created does not make too dramatic an angle change as someone walks around the area being lit.

If a number of fixtures are being used to simulate sunlight, be careful to have them coming from a similar angle so that the shadows they create are facing a fairly uniform direction as the performer moves from one fixture's focus to another's. This concern over the shadows created seems a minor detail but can add greatly to the effectiveness of the scene if carefully planned. It is one of those things that not many people will actually notice if it works properly, though it may help them become comfortable with a scene. If it doesn't work, it may distract quite a few people, even if they don't realize what is bothering them or keeping them from becoming completely involved with the scene.

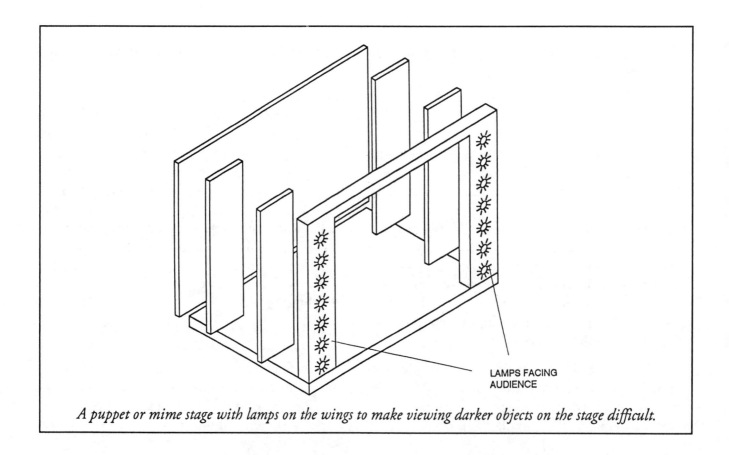

LAMPS FACING
AUDIENCE

A puppet or mime stage with lamps on the wings to make viewing darker objects on the stage difficult.

This is a subtle aspect of lighting a scene and can only be addressed completely if you have the luxury of some extra dimmers and fixtures you can use for the sunlight wash. Most often you must use a common wash to create your sunlight. At this time you should just try to keep the lighting as even as possible, both in coverage and in angle of projection.

PUPPETRY AND MIME STAGES

One effect that uses the concept of transient adaptation discussed earlier is used on many puppetry and mime stages. It involves bordering the outer edges of the stage with lamps bright enough to make it difficult for people to see dark objects on the stage, but not so bright as to be too annoying.

Using lamps of moderate brightness facing the audience, people, sticks, and various props can be concealed on stage by having them covered in black against a black background. Everything you want the audience to see you color in a very light color. Using black velour as the covering and background, you can effectively render a person or an object nvisible. By designing the covering properly the person or object can be made to appear magically on stage right before the audience's eyes. This effect has been used successfully for everything from children's puppet shows to very elaborate mime acts. You should experiment with the level of light required to mask the stage properly. Make sure you don't have it too bright for too long.

Lighting on a Budget

To every designer or technician there comes a time when what is desired does not match what is possible. More often than not the shortfall has something to do with your budget. No matter how much people do not like to think about it, money is a reality in the arts, especially the performing arts. There are some creative ways to stretch the amount of lighting effect you get out of your lighting inventory. By doing this you may be able to do the production, and your design, a great service while not doing in the producer.

CHOICE OF FIXTURES

Many of the easiest ways to stretch your lighting occur during the design layout phase of a show. One method is to choose larger lighting areas and use fixtures with wider beam spreads to cover more area with less equipment. As long as you can obtain adequate intensity levels with the fixtures this is an easy way to get by with less. It could allow you to move fixtures into assignments for added effect lighting and specials.

Choosing to use fixtures that flood a large area with light for washes can cut down on how many fixtures are needed for each wash. Scoops, floods, and some fresnels are able to adequately cover fairly large areas evenly. A couple of scoops can give a fairly even wash of light across a backdrop instead of using several striplights. You should also try not to make the stage too bright. Many fixtures have been tied up bringing a stage to 200 or more footcandles only to be dimmed down through the entire performance.

CONTROL

The most common place to fall short in equipment is control. In the chapter on control several techniques for stretching dimmers are discussed. These include replugging, A/B switching, and refocusing/regelling. All three methods are based on the same idea — getting more effect out of less dimming. Replugging and A/B switching are the same idea. They allow more than one set of instruments to be controlled by the same dimmer during different parts of the show.

Replugging and A/B Switching

With replugging, the different instruments are unplugged from the dimmers, and new ones are plugged in for when they will be needed. This can be done as many times during the show as is possible.

A/B switching is the same idea except instead of actually unplugging the instruments they are plugged into a box with more than one outlet, controlled by a switch plugged into each dimmer. Which outlet is active is determined by the position of the switch for that dimmer. You can actually switch as many instrument groups as you have positions on the switches.

Refocusing and Regelling

With replugging and A/B switching, you are taking care of a shortage of dimmers but still using the extra fixtures. With refocusing and regelling you are addressing the situation where you just don't have enough fixtures to cover all the effects needed. Refocusing is generally only carried out during intermission or during breaks between sets. At that time you must refocus instruments that are no longer needed where they are focused to focus on other subjects for parts of the rest of the show. You should try to keep the refocus as quick and simple as possible so that it doesn't interfere with anything else. Try not to make them involve actually taking a fixture down and moving it. It is best if the instrument is just aimed in a new direction.

Regelling is a very effective way to stretch the number of effects you get out of your fixtures. By changing the color the fixture projects, you can completely change the effect that it delivers. Couple regelling with any of the other instrument-sharing techniques outlined, and you can get a lot of lighting out of a fairly small inventory.

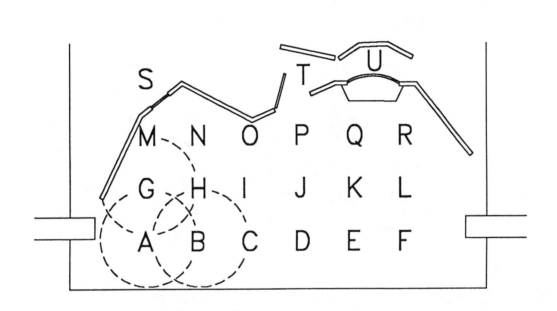

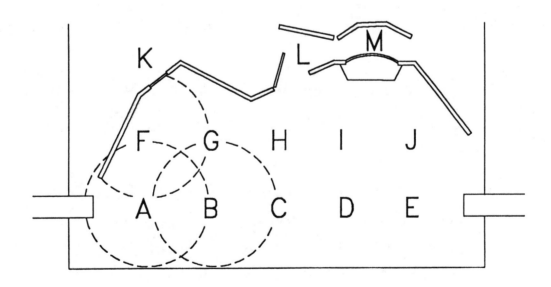

A stage layout with smaller and larger areas. Smaller areas give greater flexibility but require more instruments and dimmers.

upstage right
replugs

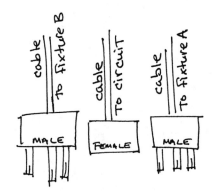

Tie each replug
bundle together
and label each
cable

Run so cables hang
4' off floor at
side wall

circuit	fixture A	fixture B
① #22	#15	#32
② #37	#'s 26,48	#12
③ #50	#63	#64

① after cue 14 change to fixture B
   at intermission change to fixture A

② after cue 27 change to fixture B
   after cue 62 change to fixture A
   after cue 81 change to fixture B
   end of show change back to fixture A

③ after cue 43 or at intermission change to
                                    fixture B

A replug layout and schedule can help increase the number of effects you can get out of your dimmers.

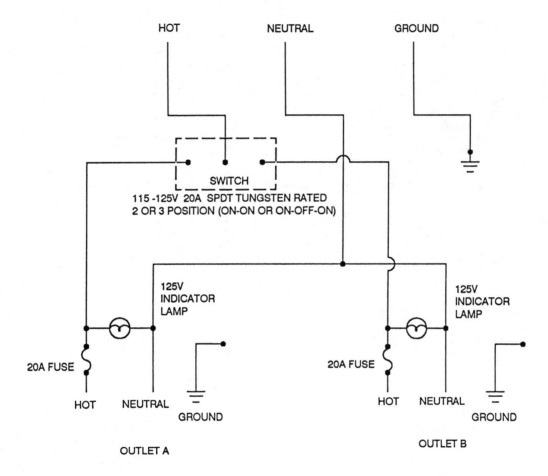

INPUT FROM POWER SUPPLY - MALE PLUG

HOT   NEUTRAL   GROUND

SWITCH
115 -125V 20A SPDT TUNGSTEN RATED
2 OR 3 POSITION (ON-ON OR ON-OFF-ON)

125V
INDICATOR
LAMP

125V
INDICATOR
LAMP

20A FUSE

20A FUSE

HOT   NEUTRAL

GROUND

HOT   NEUTRAL

GROUND

OUTLET A

OUTLET B

OUTPUTS TO LIGHTING FIXTURES - FEMALE CONNECTORS

(indicator lamps and fuses are optional)

SINGLE CIRCUIT SCHEMATIC - REPEAT FOR EACH SEPARATE INPUT
SOURCE

An A/B box schematic (SPDT) for a non-remote switch box.
If switches without a tungsten rating are used, you should not switch them while they are on.

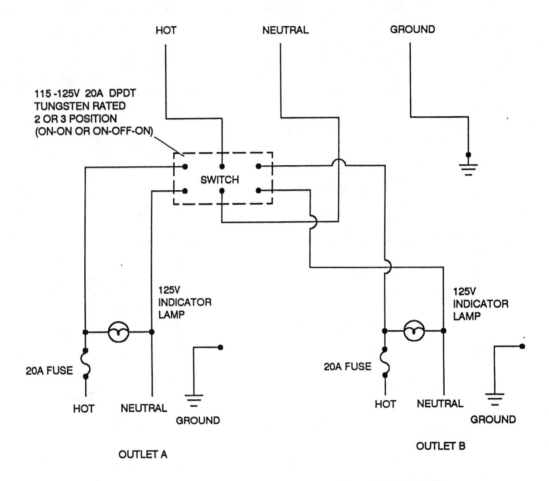

HOT & NEUTRAL SWITCHED FOR ADDED SAFETY

INPUT FROM POWER SUPPLY - MALE PLUG

HOT   NEUTRAL   GROUND

115 -125V 20A DPDT
TUNGSTEN RATED
2 OR 3 POSITION
(ON-ON OR ON-OFF-ON)

SWITCH

125V
INDICATOR
LAMP

125V
INDICATOR
LAMP

20A FUSE   20A FUSE

HOT   NEUTRAL   HOT   NEUTRAL

GROUND   GROUND

OUTLET A   OUTLET B

OUTPUTS TO LIGHTING FIXTURES - FEMALE CONNECTORS

(Indicator lamps and fuses are optional)

SINGLE CIRCUIT SCHEMATIC - REPEAT FOR EACH SEPARATE INPUT
SOURCE

An A/B box schematic (DPDT) using a double pole switch is safest
because it switches off both the hot and neutral conductors.

Documenting and Scheduling

With all the techniques that share either fixtures or dimmers, it is very important that everything be documented well and scheduled into the running of the show. If any item is not set down properly it will be forgotten and not ready when you need it. These factors also must be taken care of even if something else is going wrong, so make sure you always set enough time aside to address these tasks. Do not get too carried away with these techniques, making the running crew carry out too many tasks. Time must be set aside for a little rest as well as attending to any emergencies that come up. If you fill every minute with a task to be done, a sacrifice must be made when something unforeseen pops up.

SIMPLIFY

Another method you can use to get more for less is simplifying what you are trying to do. If a sunny day or moonlit night can be captured by a single fixture shining through a window, don't tie up several of your valuable fixtures going after the same effect. Often the most subtle suggestions of an event can create the most dramatic impressions. It is a famous and widespread belief that "less is more." Try to figure out the simplest way to do what you have to do. It will often end up being the most desirable way.

Pre-Production

The meeting is over and the lighting plot complete. The production staff is leaving the room, and you are left holding a mountain of paper conveying everything you will need to know about lighting the show. The next phase of pre-production (the time and processes that take place before a show opens) involves sitting down with all this information to plan and prepare for the load-in. This preparation *must* occur, even if the whole production staff and crew, and cast for that matter, is you. In fact, it is sometimes even more important when you are working alone, since no one else will back you up.

The next few chapters discuss the mounting, running, and closing of a show, relating the processes involved using a show with settings and various crews. The information is just as important for one person playing at a local bar and doing his own lighting as it is for a major musical with a large cast and crews to match.

Do not downplay the importance of your lighting, its preparation and execution, because your show is "so small." At the moment of performance your audience will experience your show, and no other. Work to make it the best that it possibly can be. An acoustic soloist with a very simple show can be (and generally is) a much more sincerely emotional experience than a large band complete with a technical extravaganza.

CRITICAL EVENT SCHEDULE

To keep the task ahead in control, without allowing it to become too overwhelming, you should make a *critical event schedule*. This is a listing in chart form indicating the different events, or tasks, that must occur and at what time they should be begun and completed. This could be broken down by weeks, days, or even hours, depending on which events you are charting. By creating this chart you can see what must be done before some other event can be completed. This minimizes time wasted starting something that cannot be completed until another task is completed. It also helps keep an eye on everything to keep progress going forward, and it allows you to stop worrying about some things before you need to. Knowing that you do not have to be concerned with something until another specific event is completed or a time is reached allows you to "pigeon-hole" it and forget about it until later, concentrating on what must be done *now*.

BILL OF MATERIALS

The first step of planning for the lighting part of the load-in is to make a detailed bill of materials, a listing or series of listings of everything needed to complete the lighting of the show, down to the last gel cut or C-clamp. This can be the responsibility of the lighting designer, an assistant, or an electrician responsible for preparing the lighting.

One of the hardest parts of preparing an accurate bill of materials is determining the cable runs required. If the theater or theaters in which your production will be performed do not have wiring devices with connections at the locations you will require, cable runs will be required from either the dimmers or the plug boxes. Most larger scale shows and concerts lay out exactly how the show will be hung and order multi-cables from the production houses with drops along the cable lengths wherever needed. This method is very efficient but also quite expensive. Small to medium shows more often use individual cable runs, either loose or bundled together using electrical tape (if the shows are touring and must be repeatedly loaded in and out of theaters).

In the case of a tour that will be playing theaters of widely varying sizes, the cables required for the largest house are determined, and a plan for adapting to the smaller theaters is devised. It is always a good idea to have extra cable available, whether resident or touring, in case something unforeseen occurs.

List of Fixtures

The bill of materials should include a listing of lighting fixtures to be used, generally grouped by focal length or beam angle and wattage. Connectors needed

Fixtures

	Count	Checked	Own	Rented

Ellipsoidals -

6x9 - 500W..EHD....................	18				
6x9 - 750W..EHG....................	11				
6x12- 500W..EHD....................	8				
6x12- 750W..EHG....................	17				
6x16- 750W..EHG....................	22				
6x16- 1000W.FEL....................	9				

Fresnels -

6" - 750W...BTN....................	14				
8" - 1000W..BVT....................	11				
8" - 1500W..CWZ....................	3				

PARS -

64 - 500W..MFL....................	19				
64 - 1000W.MFL.FFR..............	11				
64 - 1000W.NSP.FFP.............	12				
46 - 300W..NSP....................	9				

FLOODS -

Mini-Flood - 500W.FDN............	16				

STRIPS/CYCS -

6' Mini-Strip 50W EXZ.............	6				
6' Mini-Strip 50W EXT.............	6				
6' R40, 3ckt.150W.R/FL............	4				

Accessories

6" Pattern holders................	11				
7-1/2" Donut......................	11				
Patterns.....................see separate list					
6" 8-way barn door................	9				
8" 8-way barn door................	6				
R40 Border trunion................	4pr				
Piggy-back Mini-Strip trunion......6pr					
Single side arm w/ tee............	14				

A bill of materials checklist helps make sure all the equipment is ready for the load-in and returned to the proper place after the show closes.

Critical events schedule - Lighting

March 20	Lighting bill of materials (less gel)
March 22	Lighting package to bid at rental shops
March 27	Final light plot with last changes to BOM Gather crew lists
April 5	Contract lighting rental and purchases Final list of load-in crew & running crew
April 8	Gel list with cuts
April 9	Final hook ups and patch sheets Order gel
April 14	Receive & inspect lighting packages Cut gel, prep cable & equipment Complete cue script - lighting
April 16	Start load-in 11:30pm - load-in crew only
April 17	Running crew in at 7:30am Focus by 4:30pm Set levels 6:00pm Break all but 2 of load-in crew
April 18	Tech all day
April 19	Dress
April 20	Open
April 27	Press

A critical events schedule can help keep mounting a show on track.

on both the fixtures and cables should be noted clearly. Load-ins have been delayed because all the equipment had stage pin connectors and all the wiring devices had twist locks. The list should also include all the gel cuts grouped by color and size. All the control equipment needed, such as dimmers, control board, control cables, and switch boxes needs to be listed also.

It is a good practice to complete this listing even if you or the theater you work for own all the equipment. This makes it easier if the show is ever to be recreated in the future, after time has allowed equipment inventories to change.

After the listing is compiled, it must be decided and noted where the different equipment is coming from. If it is currently being used in another production, note where it is and make sure it will be available when you need it. If some or all of the equipment is to be supplied by a rental shop, be sure to give them a complete listing of what you will require as early as possible. They will need to know exactly what you need, when you will need it, and when you will be returning it. The further in advance you make the arrangements, the better chance you will have of getting the equipment you want without having to make substitutions. Be sure to call periodically and confirm your arrangements to keep your order current on their schedules. It is sometimes possible that shows calling in after you, but with earlier opening dates, will receive some of your equipment, leaving you with a problem. This generally only happens with shops with small inventories or poor organization.

PRIOR TO LOAD-IN

Some work should be taken care of prior to the load-in. All the gel should be cut to size and each piece marked with its color number using a china marker. Be sure to mark it off the center since the first area of a gel to burn is the center and it would not be as easy to see what color a fixture has. If the color frames are available, they should have the gel put into them. Both of these steps can save a great deal of time during the load-in.

At some time prior to the load-in, the cues should be entered into the script, score, or schedule that will be used for "calling" or "cueing" the show. Sometimes there just isn't time for any of this to be done ahead and then you have to deal with it all during the load-in. It isn't the end of the world, so don't worry, just plan for it. (It isn't even all that unusual.)

Detailing the Load-In and Crews

Once arrangements have been made for the equipment to be at the theater when you need it, it is time to detail the load-in. This is usually done together with the people responsible for the settings, costumes, and rehearsal scheduling. The size of the crew allowed and the amount of stage time available must be determined. After this task is complete, a load-in crew is gathered. Each member of the crew, whether it is one person or many, should be instructed to arrive at the theater on time and equipped with at least an 8-inch adjustable wrench, standard and Phillips screwdrivers, pliers, and wire strippers and cutters.

You should prepare an outline of what you will need done, in the order that it should be done, who you initially plan to do it. This becomes a valuable reference when people start looking for the next job while you are in the middle of some other problem. More crew time is wasted waiting for instructions than on any other item. An outline of the load-in can also be used to measure how things are going: you can compare how much is done and how much time is left. Surprises and changes are handled much more easily when an original plan exists. Otherwise, jobs have a way of being forgotten in the confusion of trying to develop a course of action while things are constantly changing.

LOAD-IN

Among the most anxious moments for a stage technician are the first few moments of the load-in. This is when all the preparation can pay off by reducing the chance of being overwhelmed by the tasks before you. If everything has been thought out fairly well beforehand, your confidence in the plan can keep things going smoothly.

A load-in generally consists of several phases. What those phases are depends on the circumstances of each production. If the stage has a show on it already, the

GO L58

The scene opens on a wooded glen at dawn. MARY, JANE, and WOODY are still sleeping near a now low fire. JENNY and SCOTT are off near a small grouping of elm talking quietly.
Their conversation seems to be a little controlled, keeping a level of anxiety as carefully checked as possible.

JENNY is looking off toward the horizon. It is a clear day and the sunrise is stunning.

JENNY: What a beautiful sunrise. I didn't expect this morning to
              seem so nice.

WARN S14

SCOTT: What did you think you would wake up to? There has
              been nothing skulking about the trail so far.

                    JENNY looks over at SCOTT

JENNY: Well...you know..I just felt that maybe... I don't know, I
              just felt a little less sure of things.

                    JENNY looks back to the horizon

WARN L59

SCOTT: Nothing has changed. The sun will continue to rise, and
              it will not pause before continuing on its journey across
              the sky. The birds will not fall silent, and there will not be
              any...

GO S14

A noise from off in the deeper woods brings SCOTT up short, quickly drawing his attention.

JENNY looks worriedly to SCOTT, concerned and at the same time embarrassed. She quickly looks away.

SCOTT realizes it was just an animal in the brush, and that his reaction was not missed.

SCOTT: ...well there won't be anything so different.

JENNY: I know, you're right. *(looking over toward the others)*
              Look at them, I have never been able to sleep so late
              outside. We may starve before they get up for breakfast.

— GO L59

The cue script, whether a script of a play or a musical score or lyric sheet,
keeps the lighting in sync with the show.

show will have to be "torn down" or loaded out before a new one can be mounted. Loading one show in immediately after loading one out is often referred to as a "changeover." This may be the responsibility of all those loading in the new show along with the closing show's crew or the responsibility of the crew involved with the closing show.

After an old show is unloaded, the load-in begins with actually loading the equipment (lighting, settings, costumes, etc.) into the theater, either from shops or trucks. After this is complete, a schedule must be followed so that the different departments involved with the show have their share of time on stage. Generally, the settings and lighting take turns working on stage, either by giving up the stage entirely for specified periods of time, or by one working upstage while the other works downstage.

Hanging Lights

It should be arranged so that the lighting may be hung without trying to work around a set. Light plots can be hung much faster on a bare stage when possible, leaving only those fixtures whose position is dependent on certain set pieces. It is often possible to quick-focus prior to some of the set being erected. It is also important for the settings to be put up without working around ladders and lighting fixtures lying around on the stage. It is nearly impossible for the lights and sets to be put up at the same time. It is often attempted but always ends in heated tempers and lost time.

When hanging the light plot, ellipsoidals should have their shutters (and irises if so equipped) opened all the way as they are hung. This prevents one from being turned on and baking its completely closed shutters while other fixtures are being focused.

Focusing

After the lights and sets are up, time is taken to focus the light plot. This should be done as efficiently as possible. Most often a fixture is not colored, or gelled, until after it is focused. After the fixture is focused and carefully locked in place by tightening the appropriate bolts and knobs, the color frame with its gel in place (this should have been prepared prior to the load-in)

is put in the fixture's color frame holder. The most common method of focusing is to have either the lighting designer or his assistant on stage calling instructions to one or more electricians who handle the fixtures. (One often used request is to "flag" the fixture. This means to wave your hand in front of it so that its beam can be distinguished from others on the same circuit.)

Many designers stand in the position they want the light focused and have the beam placed on them. Others have another person stand in place so that they can look at the light on the person. This also saves their eyes from having to look into the bright lights, making it difficult to see what they are doing. Often the brightest spot of the fixture — the hot spot — is aimed at the target person's chest to allow full coverage of the body.

Setting Cues and Levels

After focusing and making any adjustments to the set, it is necessary to schedule a good deal of time for setting cues and levels. At this point, the designer needs to be able to see the stage set as it will be during a scene so that the different levels of the control channels, or dimmers, may be set up. This must be determined and noted for each cue.

Technical and Dress Rehearsals

After levels are set, technical rehearsals are required for the electricians, carpenters, properties people, and costumers to learn the show. The next rehearsal is the perennially problematic dress rehearsal — the rehearsal with full lights, costumes, sets, and props before the opening performance. An interesting note is that there never seems to be enough time for all these processes to be carried out to the point of everyone being comfortable with them. Whether you load in to a matinee today or have a week to load in and rehearse, it always seems that another day or two would just smooth things out perfectly. Though it is not an official practice it does seem fairly universal that you go out to a twenty-four-hour diner after the load-in is complete and have breakfast, no matter what time of day or night you finish.

Load-in Checklist - Lighting
Page 1 of 3

Before load-in starts:

Fixtures checked

Gel cut

Cable checked

Frames stuffed

Crew in at 11:00pm

After load-in begins:

Strip FOH

Check FOH fixtures

Strip stage electrics

Check stage fixtures

Clear patch

Set new patch

Hang FOH

Hang 1st electric

Hang 2nd electric

Hang 3rd electric

Hang 4th electric

Focus FOH

Focus stage electrics

A load-in checklist helps when organizing what has to happen.

Preliminary Load-in Schedule - Lighting

11:00pm	Load-in crew in
11:30pm	3 drop FOH, rest bring in new equipment and crates for old
12:00am	Strip all stage electrics, 2 check FOH fixtures
2:30am	Off stage for 1 hr for sets, 3 hang FOH while rest check equipment from stage electrics
3:30am	Hang 1st and 2nd electric
4:30am	Hang 3rd and 4th electric
5:30am	Focus FOH
6:00am	Running crew in Focus 1st and 2nd electrics
7:00am	Focus 3rd and 4th electrics
8:00am	Load-in crew off Cleanup
9:30am	Wire practicals on set
12:00pm	Lunch
2:30pm	Set levels rest final cleanup
5:00pm	Dinner
6:00pm	Tech rehearsal

A load-in tentative schedule can help determine how much time each task should take.

Production

After the show is in and rehearsed, it is time for performances. At this point, how every item is to be carried out should be well defined. Generally, the crew must arrive either an hour before the performance begins (curtain time or just "curtain") or a half hour before curtain (known simply as "half hour"), depending on the choice of management. At a set time everyone must get in place to run the show. How the show is actually run varies. Most shows have a stage manager "calling the show," which means telling the various crews when to get ready and when to carry out a cue. Sometimes the person running the lighting control board will call the lighting cues, with the set crew (carpenters) cued independently. There are times everyone on the crew is responsible for his or her own cues taking place at the right time. This method can get a little chaotic and is very poor for larger shows with a lot happening at one time. It has worked for many small to medium theaters putting on fairly complex shows, but not without pain and careful planning.

WORKING TOGETHER

It is important that everyone associated with a show respect all the other jobs involved. Live performances are a collaboration of many talents, and no one talent is more important than others. Try to keep in mind how what you are doing may affect what someone else is trying to do. This consideration may help avoid many conflicts and may win you some respect.

WHEN SOMETHING GOES WRONG

At some point something is going to go wrong during a performance. You will appreciate planning ahead and making contingency plans. Determine which fixtures or channels in a plot could be added to a cue in the event that a key light burns out during a performance. Decide what to do if a bank of dimmers fails. Have a backup plan for when the normal control board fails and either a backup section or board must be

used. If backup control is not available, what else can be done to get the show running? Forget about the fact that any plan will compromise the lighting of the show; that is an obvious result of a problem occurring. Just get the show up and running as quickly as possible with the best compromise. This is done by determining the best solutions to as many problems as you can think of that might occur.

Trying to think up creative solutions to some of the things that can happen is tough when you are under the time pressures involved with live performances. Sometimes improvising can't be avoided; however, a little forethought can turn a catastrophe into a mere inconvenience.

LIGHT CHECK

After the show is up and running it should be kept running as if the plot were just hung. Either before or after each performance, whichever time allows you to work for a while without being seen by the audience, a light check should be carried out. Walking around on stage, working in view of the audience, is considered unprofessional and in poor taste. During the check all the lights should be brought up to about half intensity so that it is easy to check for lamp outages and gels that need replacement. Do not wait until the plot is missing several fixtures or the show just doesn't seem to have the same feel it used to before doing anything.

EQUIPMENT CHECK

At set intervals, maybe every few performances or once a week, the fixtures, cabling, and control equipment should be checked for wear and cleaned. Connections should be made sure and controls and switches cleaned to prevent dirt (or carbon) from building up. If you use the equipment over a long term — months, for instance — you will have to set up a schedule periodically to pull some fixtures down, completely clean them, align or adjust them, and rehang them. It is not

Emergency Cues
Page 1 of 7

To use 12 channel back-up board
patch the following into dimmers 25-36 or 37-48
and tie board into the pack selected (1 = 25 or 36, 2 = 26 or 37...)

1 - 1,6,12,26,29,35,39,42   - Front (FOH) warm
2 - 2,7,13,27,31,38,45,53   - Front (FOH) cool
3 - 62,75,79,84,88,97,102,111   - Front (stage) warm
4 - 64,78,85,86,93,101,108,114   - Front (stage) cool
5 - 21,28,37,41   - sun wash (full stage)
6 - 23,32,36,44   - moon wash (full stage)
7 - 16,25   - couch special
8 - 4,34,48   - bar special
9 - 65   - window special
10 - 71,81   - "red" cyc
11 - 72,82   - "blue" cyc
12 - 73,83   - "green" cyc

<u>cue</u>

1 - 1^2 2^4 3^3 4^5 6^6 10^2 11^4 12^2

2 - $1\uparrow^4$ $2\uparrow^6$ $3\uparrow^4$ $4\uparrow^7$ $5\uparrow^3$

3 - $8\uparrow^6$

4 - 15 count to black

A backup cue sheet should be put together before it is needed.

Lighting production maintenance schedule

Prior to each show:

Lamp check

Weekly:

SUN	- focus clean up
WED, SAT	- gel check

Monthly:

1st THURS   - tune & clean FOH inst.
                check cable

2nd THURS   - tune & clean 1st & 2nd electrics' inst.
                check cable

3rd THURS   - tune & clean 3rd & 4th electrics' inst.
                check cable

4th THURS   - tune & clean dimming & control
                check patch & control cabling

Annual:

FEB, AUG,   - have control board serviced and cleaned

A show maintenance schedule keeps the equipment in proper working order
and the show looking like opening night.

a good idea to leave them hanging from show to show without some kind of preventative maintenance.

Taking the time to do all this regularly will keep the show running smoothly with the look of a new show and will keep the equipment in good shape. If you or the theater you work for own the equipment, it makes sense to protect the investment. If the equipment is rented, it will win you some excellent support in the future if the equipment is returned in good shape without signs of abuse or neglect. A shop will be more willing to go a little further for you or rush a little more when you need it if they know you respect and care for their equipment.

Post-Production

Before the final performance, a meeting should be held to plan for the load-out. If there is a show being loaded right into the theater after the current one is loaded out the meeting should discuss the load-in as well. It is usually best to take the scenery down before starting to take down the lighting. This way the lighting can be dropped onto a bare stage.

PROPER STORAGE IS ESSENTIAL

Though time is always tight it cannot be stressed enough how important it is that the equipment not being used for the next show be taken down carefully and stored properly. Ellipsoidals should have their shutters pushed all the way in to prevent their bending. Gel should be pulled from the fixtures and discarded if it shows any signs of fading; the color frames packed by size. Any patterns in the ellipsoidals should be removed and, if in good shape, stored for future use. Cable must be carefully coiled, tied off, and packed away. All tape, ties, and markings put on the equipment for the show should be removed. If any of the equipment was in special containers, it should be repacked in them.

After all the equipment is down and packed, it should be carefully stored or set aside to be returned to wherever it came from. Many times an order put together promptly by a rental shop to meet a show's deadline is kept sitting around the theater after the show closes, waiting to be returned. A shop must check out and rework the equipment before it can be put back into rental stock. The time it sits around in your theater costs you money and some other show precious time.

TIME TO CELEBRATE!

After everything is done and whatever needs to be stored is put away it is time to go out and celebrate. Two of the greatest moments experienced when working on live performances are when you load a show in

and it opens successfully, and when you finish loading out a show that has had a successful run. Sometimes, when a changeover occurs, both happen at the same time and after the dust settles it can feel great. Beginnings and endings, when everything is planned carefully and carried out well, are when the most excitement can be experienced. It is because of those moments that most people involved with putting on shows keep coming back for more.

Load-out - Lighting
Page 1 of 2

Prior to final curtain:

Clear space for staging and storage of equipment

Prep any storage or transport containers

Crew arrives 9:30pm

Load-out begins:

Drop FOH fixtures and cable

Drop & strip 1st & 2nd electric

Drop & strip 3rd & 4th electric

Separate rented equipment to be returned

Separate owned equipment to be stored from owned equipment used in next show

Pack rental equipment being returned

Pack owned equipment to be stored

Prep equipment being re-hung for next show

A load-out checklist helps keep the load-out flowing smoothly.

Glossary

ACCENT WASH — A wash of light over an area, adding color.

ACL LIGHT — A narrow beam, low voltage PAR aircraft landing light.

ADAPTATION — The process of the eye getting used to or reacting to changes in light intensity.

AMPERAGE — A component of electricity used to measure the number of electrons moving past a given point in a circuit.

ANSI — American National Standards Institute.

AREA LIGHTING — The main visibility lighting for an acting area.

BARN DOOR — A device with two or four doors for masking a light beam off areas.

BATTEN — A pipe hung from the grid or ceiling.

BEAM ANGLE — The angle at which the beam edges are 50% of the center beam candlepower.

BEAM SPREAD FACTOR — A number with which you multiply the throw distance to determine beam spread.

BLACKOUT — The fast shutdown of all lighting.

BLIND MODE — Setting up a lighting scene or preset when another is active.

BOOM — A vertical pipe mounted in a base, used to hang lighting fixtures.

BORDER — See STRIPLIGHT.

BULB — The "glass" part of a lamp.

CANDELA — A unit measuring the intensity of light.

CANDLEPOWER — A term used in place of "intensity."

COLOR TEMPERATURE — A factor given for lamps, comparing their color to that of a "blackbody" at a given temperature.

CONTROL BOARD — A remote device used to control dimmers.

CROSS FADE — To fade from one scene to another.

CROSS FADER — A control for fading from one preset scene to another.

CUE — A change in the lighting.

CYC — Short for "cyclorama." A drop used to create the illusion of infinite space.

DARK ADAPTATION — The process of the eye adapting to changes from light to dark.

DELTA SYSTEM — An electrical configuration (3ø) with a "high" center leg.

DIM — To lower the amount of voltage to a fixture, thereby decreasing its light output.

DIMMER — A device used to control how much voltage is supplied to a lighting fixture.

DOWNSTAGE — The area on stage closest to the audience.

DROP BOX — A plug box that can be dropped where it is needed.

EFFECT — An event or a moment intended to create a particular emotional reaction.

EFFECT LIGHTING — Lighting intended to create a mood or an impression.

EFFECT WASH — Effect lighting covering a broad area.

ELLIPSOIDAL — Spotlight that uses an ellipsoidal reflector.

FIELD ANGLE — The angle at which the beam edges are 10% of the center beam candlepower.

FIXTURE — A lighting unit, or luminaire.

FLAG — To wave an object or a hand in front of an instrument to determine its coverage area.

FLOOR POCKET — A wiring device with receptacles recessed into the floor and a hinged cover.

FOCUS — To aim a lighting fixture, or to adjust a fixture's beam.

FOCUSING INSTRUMENT — A lighting instrument whose beam can be varied and controlled.

FOLLOWSPOT — A lighting instrument used to follow a performer on stage.

FOOTCANDLE — A unit of illumination. 1 footcandle = 1 lumen/ft^2.

FRESNEL — A lighting instrument using a fresnel lens.

FRONT LIGHT — A light coming from downstage of the subject, generally brought in 45° off full front.

GEL — A plastic color media for modifying a beam of light.

GOBO — A silhouette pattern used to project images from an ellipsoidal spotlight.

GRID — The structure above the stage, usually used to support the battens.

HOT PATCHING — Putting a circuit into a dimmer while it is on. NOT RECOMMENDED.

HOUSE POSITION — A lighting position located in the audience.

INDEPENDENT SWITCHES — The controls on a lighting control board that allow independent control of a channel.

INSTRUMENT — A lighting unit.

JUMPER — A cable or an extension cord used to tie an outlet to a plug.

LAMP — The complete assembly of a bulb, filament, base, etc.

LIGHT ADAPTATION — The process of the eye adapting to changes from dark to light.

LOAD — The lamp or lighting instruments placed on a circuit.

LUMEN — A unit of light flux.

MASK — To hide from view.

MODEL — To use light and shadow to enhance three-dimensionality.

MULTIPLE PAGES — Different sets of memory for a single control.

NON-DIM — A circuit switched full on to full off, as with a traditional switch.

PAR — Parabolic Aluminized Reflector, a lamp or lighting unit.

PATCH — Tying a circuit into a dimmer or a dimmer into a control channel.

PINSPOT — A fixture providing a narrow beam of light.

PRACTICAL — A working light mounted on a set piece, such as a working sconce.

PRESET SCENE — A bank of potentiometers used to preset a lighting scene.

RAINLIGHT — A pinspot using a low voltage, narrow beam lamp.

ROUNDEL — A round glass lens used to color striplights.

SATURATED — A color containing a high percentage of one primary color is considered "saturated."

SCOOP — A flood light using a large scoop-shaped reflector.

SET WASH — A wash of light used to light the setting.

SIDEARM — A pipe and C-clamp arrangement used to hang a lighting fixture.

SLIDING TEE — A coupling used to hang a lighting fixture from ½-inch IP pipe.

SOFT PATCH — Plugging dimmers into control channels electronically.

SPECIAL — A fixture used for one specific object or effect.

SPLIT FADER — A cross fader capable of bringing up both presets at once.

STAGE LEFT — The actor's left as he faces the audience.

STAGE RIGHT — The actor's right as he faces the audience.

STRIPLIGHT — A strip of sockets in a single fixture. Also, borderlight.

THROW DISTANCE — The distance from a lighting fixture to the object being lit.

TORMENTOR — A wall-mounted pipe for mounting lighting fixtures.

TRANSIENT ADAPTATION — The process of the eye adapting from viewing an area at one level of light to an area of higher or lower level.

TRIM HEIGHT — The height from the stage floor at which a batten is set.

UPSTAGE — The area on stage farthest from the audience.

VISIBILITY LIGHTING — The lighting used to allow the audience to see the action on stage.

VOLTAGE — The unit used to measure the difference in charge between the most positive and most negative points in a circuit.

WASH — A light or group of lights covering a broad area.

WATTAGE — The power consumed by a circuit.

WIRING DEVICE — The equipment used to distribute electricity.

X-RAY — See STRIPLIGHT.

Appendices

1. Common Lighting Symbols

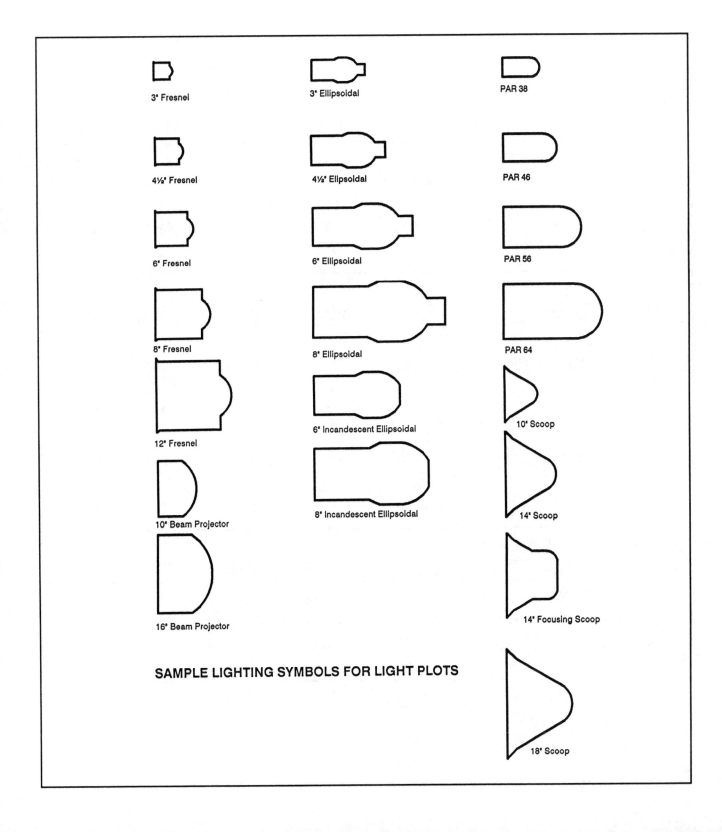

3" Fresnel

3" Ellipsoidal

PAR 38

4½" Fresnel

4½" Ellipsoidal

PAR 46

6" Fresnel

6" Ellipsoidal

PAR 56

8" Fresnel

8" Ellipsoidal

PAR 64

12" Fresnel

6" Incandescent Ellipsoidal

10" Scoop

10" Beam Projector

8" Incandescent Ellipsoidal

14" Scoop

16" Beam Projector

14" Focusing Scoop

SAMPLE LIGHTING SYMBOLS FOR LIGHT PLOTS

18" Scoop

2. Common Fixture Photometrics

Ellipsoidals

FOCAL LENGTH	LAMP	CBCP	BEAM	MF	FIELD	MF
4½ x 6½	750W EHG	38,250	26°	0.46	50°	0.93
6 x 9		66,000	19°	0.34	40°	0.73
6 x 12		115,500	14°	0.25	29°	0.52
6 x 16		141,000	10°	0.18	19°	0.34
6 x 22		164,250	7°	0.12	11°	0.19

Fresnels

SIZE	LAMP	CBCP	BEAM	MF	FIELD	MF
6"	750W BTN	Flood 13,500	50°	0.93	64°	1.25
		Spot 83,250	7°	0.12	16°	0.28
8"	1000W BVT	Flood 24,800	52°	0.98	64°	1.25
		Spot 114,000	9°	0.16	19°	0.34

PARS (and PAR or R type borders)

SIZE	LAMP		CBCP	FIELD	MF
64	1KW	VNSP(FFN)	400,000	10°x24°	0.18x0.42
all 1K lamps		NSP (FFP)	330,000	14°x26°	0.25x0.46
given 3200°K		MFL (FFR)	125,000	21°x44°	0.37x0.81
		WFL (FFS)	40,000	45°x71°	0.83x1.43
	500W	VNSP	203,000	8°x20°	0.14x0.35
		NSP	117,000	13°x20°	0.23x0.35
		MFL	40,600	20°x35°	0.35x0.63
		WFL	12,700	35°x65°	0.63x1.27

PARS (and PAR or R type borders)						
SIZE	LAMP		CBCP	FIELD	MF	
Reflector Kit 3200°K	600W	DYS	266,000	14°	0.24	
56	500W	NSP	94,500	15°x32°	0.26x0.57	
		MFL	47,800	20°x42°	0.35x0.77	
		WFL	18,300	34°x66°	0.61x1.30	
	300W	NSP	72,400	15°x20°	0.26x0.35	
		MFL	25,400	20°x35°	0.35x0.63	
		WFL	11,200	30°x60°	0.54x1.15	
46	200W	NSP	34,600	17°x23°	0.30x0.4	
		MFL	12,500	22°x39°	0.39x0.71	
38	150W	R/FL	3,600	60°	1.15	
		R/SP	11,000	30°	0.54	
	250W	PAR/FL	6,500	35°	0.63	
		PAR/SP	28,000	24°	0.43	
	300W	R/FL	2,900	120°	3.46	
		R/SP	14,000	40°	0.73	
36 RAIN	4515	6.4V 30W	55,000	5°	0.09	
46 RAIN	4535	6.4V 30W	95,000	4°x5.5°	0.07x0.10	
36 ACL	4594	28V 100W	70,000	13°x7°	0.23x0.12	
	4596	28V 250W	150,000	11°x12°	0.19x0.21	
46 ACL	4553	28V 250W	300,000	11°x12°	0.19x0.21	

Scoops							
SIZE	LAMP		CBCP	BEAM	MF	FIELD	MF
10"	250W	G/FL	2180	75°	1.54	108°	2.75
		G/SP	2700	75°	1.54	108°	2.75
	400W	G/FL	4075	75°	1.54	108°	2.75
		G/SP	5050	75°	1.54	108°	2.75

Scoops

SIZE	LAMP		CBCP	BEAM	MF	FIELD	MF
14" FOCUSING	1000W EGJ		Flood 18,500	68°	1.35	105°	2.61
			Med. Flood 23,500	34°	0.61	90°	2.00
14"	1000W		5,400	85°	1.83	125°	3.80
18"	1000W		12,000	80°	1.68	110°	2.86

Borders/Striplights

TYPE	LAMP		CBCP	BEAM horizontal	MF horizontal	FIELD horizontal	MF horizontal
Cyc Strip	300W	EHM	6000	49°	.91	72°	1.45
		EHZ*	5700				
	500W	FDF	13250				
		FDN*	12500				
		FCL	10000				
		FCZ*	9300	* inside frosted			
	750W	EJG	20000				
		EMD*	19500				
	1000W	FCM	27500				
		FHM*	26000				
Mini-Strip	50W	EXT	19000	14°	.25	24°	.42
		EXZ	5400	27°	.48	49°	.91
		EXN	3000	40°	.73	64°	1.25
	65W	FPA	22000	14°	.25	30°	.54
		FPC	9000	27°	.48	40°	.73
		FPB	4000	38°	.69	51°	.95
	75W	EYF	24600	14°	.25	24°	.42
		EYJ	9200	25°	.44	35°	.63
		EYC	4200	42°	.77	64°	1.25

3. Multiplying Factor Chart

throw distance x mf = beam diameter at subject

Angle	mf	Angle	mf	Angle	mf	Angle	mf
1.00	0.017	26.00	0.462	51.00	0.954	76.00	1.563
2.00	0.035	27.00	0.480	52.00	0.975	77.00	1.591
3.00	0.052	28.00	0.499	53.00	0.997	78.00	1.620
4.00	0.070	29.00	0.517	54.00	1.019	79.00	1.649
5.00	0.087	30.00	0.536	55.00	1.041	80.00	1.678
6.00	0.105	31.00	0.555	56.00	1.063	81.00	1.708
7.00	0.122	32.00	0.573	57.00	1.086	82.00	1.739
8.00	0.140	33.00	0.592	58.00	1.109	83.00	1.769
9.00	0.157	34.00	0.611	59.00	1.132	84.00	1.801
10.00	0.175	35.00	0.631	60.00	1.155	85.00	1.833
11.00	0.193	36.00	0.650	61.00	1.178	86.00	1.865
12.00	0.210	37.00	0.669	62.00	1.202	87.00	1.898
13.00	0.228	38.00	0.689	63.00	1.226	88.00	1.931
14.00	0.246	39.00	0.708	64.00	1.250	89.00	1.965
15.00	0.263	40.00	0.728	65.00	1.274	90.00	2.000
16.00	0.281	41.00	0.748	66.00	1.299	91.00	2.035
17.00	0.299	42.00	0.768	67.00	1.324	92.00	2.071
18.00	0.317	43.00	0.788	68.00	1.349	93.00	2.108
19.00	0.335	44.00	0.808	69.00	1.375	94.00	2.145
20.00	0.353	45.00	0.828	70.00	1.400	95.00	2.183
21.00	0.371	46.00	0.849	71.00	1.427	96.00	2.221
22.00	0.389	47.00	0.870	72.00	1.453	97.00	2.261
23.00	0.407	48.00	0.890	73.00	1.480	98.00	2.301
24.00	0.425	49.00	0.911	74.00	1.507	99.00	2.342
25.00	0.443	50.00	0.933	75.00	1.535	100.00	2.384

The above multiplying factors were developed using the formula:

$$mf = 2 \times \tan(\text{angle}/2)$$

4. Cable Ampacities

Amperage capacities of cable commonly used on stage:
(check National Electrical Code for changes)

Type SO, SJ, SJO

Gauge	Amperage
18	10
16	13
14	18
12	25
10	30
8	40
6	55
4	70
2	95

Type W, G

Gauge	Single conductor	Multi conductor
8	60	48
6	80	63
4	105	84
3	120	99
2	140	112
1	165	131
1/0	195	151
2/0	225	174
3/0	260	201
4/0	300	232

5. Common Connector Wiring Diagrams

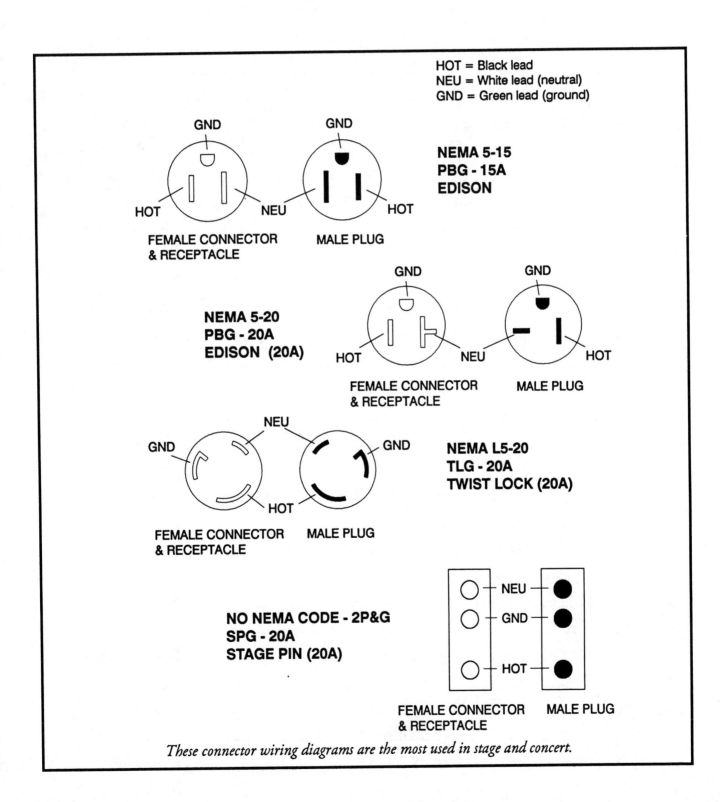

HOT = Black lead
NEU = White lead (neutral)
GND = Green lead (ground)

GND

GND

NEMA 5-15
PBG - 15A
EDISON

HOT   NEU   HOT

FEMALE CONNECTOR
& RECEPTACLE

MALE PLUG

GND

GND

NEMA 5-20
PBG - 20A
EDISON (20A)

HOT   NEU   HOT

FEMALE CONNECTOR
& RECEPTACLE

MALE PLUG

NEU

GND

GND

HOT

NEMA L5-20
TLG - 20A
TWIST LOCK (20A)

FEMALE CONNECTOR
& RECEPTACLE

MALE PLUG

NO NEMA CODE - 2P&G
SPG - 20A
STAGE PIN (20A)

NEU

GND

HOT

FEMALE CONNECTOR
& RECEPTACLE

MALE PLUG

These connector wiring diagrams are the most used in stage and concert.

6. Gel Comparisons and Descriptions

Roscolux to Lee Filters

LUX	LEE	LENE	TEMP	COMMON USES	DESCRIPTION
00	130		Neutral		Clear
01	176	802	Warm	Area, Strong Sunlight	Light Bastard Amber
02	162	803	Warm	Area, Enhances Skin Tones	Bastard Amber
03			Warm	Area, Enhances Skin Tones	Dark Bastard Amber
04	004	803	Warm	Area, Natural Sunlight	Medium Bastard Amber
05	154		Warm	Area, Gives Skin "Rosy" Look	Rose Tint
06	159	804	Warm	Area, Interiors	No Color Straw
07	007		Warm	Area, Interiors	Pale Yellow
08	103	808	Warm	Areas, Enhances Skin Tones	Pale Gold
09	009		Warm	Area, Late Afternoon Sunsets	Pale Amber Gold
10	010		Warm	Special Effects, Not For Area	Medium Yellow
11	102		Warm	Effect, Area, Bright Day, Candles	Light Straw
12	010	806	Warm	Effect, Special Effects	Straw
13	013	806	Warm	Effect, Hot Sunlit Day, Candles	Straw Tint
14	104		Warm	Effect, Sunlight	Medium Straw
15	015	809	Warm	Effect, Candle/Fire	Deep Straw
16			Warm	Area, Good for Most Skin Tones	Light Amber
17	147		Warm	Area, Tinting Washes	Light Flame
18	147	811	Warm	Effect, Afternoon Sun	Flame
19	019		Warm	Special Effect, Fire	Fire
19	164		Warm	Special Effect, Fire	Fire
20	020		Warm	Effect, Afternoon Sun, Lamp	Medium Amber
21		817	Warm	Effect, Cyc, Late Sunset	Golden Amber
22	020		Warm	Cyc, Back Lighting	Deep Amber
23	158	817	Warm	Effect, Romantic Sunlight	Orange
24	024		Warm	Special Effects, Backlight	Scarlet
25	164	818	Warm	Effect, Sunlight	Orange Red

LUX	LEE	LENE	TEMP	COMMON USES	DESCRIPTION
26	026		Warm	Effect, Near Primary	Light Red
26	106	821	Warm	Effect, Near Primary	Light Red
26	182	819	Warm	Sunlight, Near Primary	Light Red
27	027	823	Warm	Cyc, Primary	Medium Red
30	176		Warm	Area, Warms Skin Tones	Light Salmon Pink
31	107	826	Warm	Area, General Washes	Salmon Pink
32	157	830	Warm	Effect	Medium Salmon Pink
32	193		Warm	Effect	Medium Salmon Pink
33	248	825	Warm	Area, Bright — Musicals	No Color Pink
34	107	826	Warm	Area	Flesh Pink
35	035		Warm	Area	Light Pink
36	036		Warm	Area	Medium Pink
37			Warm	Area	Pale Rose Pink
38			Warm	Area	Light Rose
40	008		Warm	Effect, Sunsets	Light Salmon
41			Warm	Special Effects	Salmon
42	113		Warm	Special Effects	Deep Salmon
43			Warm	Effect	Deep Pink
44		827	Warm	Effect	Middle Rose
45		832	Warm	Toning, Background & Set Wash	Rose
46	046		Warm	Toning, Background & Set Wash	Magenta
47			Warm	Effect, Eerie Moods	Light Rose Purple
48			Warm	Effect, Pale Evenings	Rose Purple
49		126	Warm	Toning, Color Wash	Medium Purple
50	127	836	Warm	Effect, Subdued Sunlight	Mauve
51		840	Neutral	Area	Surprise Pink
52	052	840	Neutral	Area, General Washes	Light Lavender
53	053		Neutral	Area	Pale Lavender
54		843	Neutral	Area, General Wash — Tinting	Special Lavender
55	137		Neutral	Area	Lilac
57	194	841	Neutral	Area, Night Scenes	Gypsy Lavender
58	058	842	Neutral	Area, Night Scenes	Deep Lavender

LUX	LEE	LENE	TEMP	COMMON USES	DESCRIPTION
59	181		Warm	Effect, Cyc, Bold Washes	Indigo
60	202		Cool	Area	No Color Blue
61	061		Cool	Area	Mist Blue
62			Cool	Area	Booster Blue
63	063		Cool	Area	Pale Blue
64	174		Cool	Area, Realistic Moonlight	Light Steel Blue
64	161		Cool	Area, Realistic Moonlight	Light Steel Blue
65	196		Cool	Area, Dull Sky, Somber Moods	Daylight Blue
66		848	Cool	Area, Moonlight	Cool Blue
67	161	852	Cool	Area, Cyc, Excellent Sky Color	Light Sky Blue
67	165	851	Cool	Area, Cyc, Excellent Sky Color	Light Sky Blue
68	068	856	Cool	Effect, Cyc, Morning Sky Tones	Sky Blue
69	141	858	Cool	Effect, Cyc, Moonlight	Brilliant Blue
70	117	849	Cool	Area, Light Midday Skies	Nile Blue
71		853	Cool	Area, Light Midday Sky	Sea Blue
72	144		Cool	Area, Light Midday Sky	Azure Blue
73	115		Cool	Effect, Moonlight & Water	Peacock Blue
74	119		Cool	Cyc	Night Blue
76		858	Cool	Effect, Cyc, Romantic Moonlight	Light Green Blue
77		859	Cool	Effect, Cyc, Romantic Moonlight	Green Blue
78			Cool	Area, Night Scenes	Trudy Blue
79	079		Cool	Special Effects	Bright Blue
80	079	857	Cool	Cyc, Effects	Primary Blue
81			Cool	Effect, Cyc, Cold	Urban Blue
82	197		Cool	Effect	Surprise Blue
83	195	863	Cool	Cyc, Non-Realistic Night Sky	Medium Blue
84			Cool	Area, Night Scenes	Zephyr Blue
85	120	866	Cool	Cyc, Non-Realistic Night Sky	Deep Blue
86	121		Cool	Effect, Foliage, Forest Effect	Pea Green
87	245		Cool	Effect, Sunny Spring Morning	Pale Yellow Green
88	138		Neutral	Effect, Sunny Spring Morning	Light Green
89	089	871	Cool	Effect, Foliage, Mystery	Moss Green

LUX	LEE	LENE	TEMP	COMMON USES	DESCRIPTION
90	090	871	Warm	Cyc, Alternate Primary	Dark Yellow Green
91			Neutral	Cyc, Effect	Primary Green
92			Cool	Effect, Mysterious Moods	Turquoise
93			Cool	Effect, Mystery	Blue Green
94			Cool	Effect, Abstract Effects	Kelly Green
95	116	877	Cool	Cyc, Foliage in Moonlight	Medium Blue Green
97	209	880	Neutral	Reduce Color Brightness 1 Stop	Light Grey
98	210		Neutral	Reduce Color Brightness 2 Stops	Medium Grey
99	156	882	Warm	Area, Warms/Reduces Intensity	Chocolate
100		801	Neutral	Minimum Spread	Frost
101	253		Neutral	Minimum Spread	Light Frost
102	250		Warm	Moderate Spread	Light Tough Frost
103	129		Warm	Moderate Spread	Tough Frost
103	216		Warm	Moderate Spread	Tough Frost
104	228		Neutral	Moderate Spread One Direction	Tough Silk
105	214		Neutral	Minimum Spread, Reduced Intensity	Tough Spun
106	215		Neutral	Minimum Spread, Reduced Intensity	Light Tough Spun
107			Cool	Moderate Spread	Cool Frost
108	224		Cool	Moderate Spread	Daylight Frost
109			Cool	Moderate Spread One Direction	Cool Silk
111	129		Neutral	Maximum Spread	Tough Rolux
113			Neutral	Moderate Spread One Direction, Minimum Other	Matte Silk
114	253		Neutral	Lightest Spread	Hamburg Frost
120			Warm	Red Moderate Spread	Red Diffusion
121			Cool	Blue Moderate Spread	Blue Diffusion
122			Cool	Green Moderate Spread	Green Diffusion
123			Warm	Amber Moderate Spread	Amber Diffusion

Lee Filters to Roscolux

LUX	LEE	LENE	TEMP	COMMON USES	DESCRIPTION
07	007		Warm	Area, Interiors	Pale Yellow
40	008		Warm	Effect, Sunsets	Light Salmon
09	009		Warm	Area, Late Afternoon Sunsets	Pale Amber Gold
10	010		Warm	Special Effects, Not for Area	Medium Yellow
12	010		Warm	Effect, Special Effects	Straw
13	013	806	Warm	Effect, Hot Sunlit Day, Candles	Straw Tint
15	015	809	Warm	Effect, Candle/Fire	Deep Straw
19	019		Warm	Special Effect/Fire	Fire
20	020		Warm	Effect, Afternoon Sun, Lamp	Medium Amber
22	022		Warm	Cyc, Backlighting	Deep Amber
24	024		Warm	Special Effects, Backlight	Scarlet
26	026	821	Warm	Effect, Near Primary	Light Red
27	027	823	Warm	Cyc, Primary	Medium Red
35	035		Warm	Area	Light Pink
36	036		Warm	Area	Medium Pink
46	046		Warm	Toning, Background & Set Wash	Magenta
48	048		Warm	Effect, Pale Evenings	Rose Purple
52	052		Neutral	Area, General Washes	Light Lavender
53	053		Neutral	Area	Pale Lavender
61	061		Cool	Area	Mist Blue
63	063		Cool	Area	Pale Blue
68	068	856	Cool	Effect, Cyc, Morning Sky Tones	Sky Blue
79	079		Cool	Special Effects	Bright Blue
80	079	857	Cool	Cyc Effects	Primary Blue
89	089		Cool	Effect, Foliage, Mystery	Moss Green
90	090	871	Warm	Cyc, Alternate Primary	Dark Yellow Green
	101	806	Warm	Effect, Special Effects	Straw
11	102		Warm	Effect, Area, Bright Day, Candles	Light Straw
08	103	808	Warm	Areas, Enhances Skin Tones	Pale Gold
14	104		Warm	Effect, Sunlight	Medium Straw
	105		Warm	Effect, Sunlight	Amber

LUX	LEE	LENE	TEMP	COMMON USES	DESCRIPTION
26	106	821	Warm	Cyc, Near Primary	Light Red
31	107	826	Warm	Area, General Washes	Salmon Pink
34	107	826	Warm	Area	Flesh
	109	835	Warm	Effect	Medium Salmon Pink
	111		Warm	Effect	Middle Rose
42	113		Warm	Special Effects	Salmon
45	113	832	Warm	Toning, Background & Set Wash	Rose
73	115		Cool	Effect, Moonlight & Water	Peacock Blue
95	116	877	Cool	Cyc, Foliage in Moonlight	Medium Blue Green
70	117	849	Cool	Area, Light Midday Skies	Nile Blue
74	119		Cool	Cyc	Night Blue
85	120	866	Cool	Cyc, Non-Realistic Night Sky	Deep Blue
86	121		Cool	Effect, Foliage, Forest Effect	Pea Green
	122		Cool	Effect, Foliage in Bright Sun	Fern Green
	124	871	Warm	Cyc, Alternate Primary	Dark Yellow Green
49	126		Warm	Toning, Color Wash	Medium Purple
50	127	836	Warm	Effect, Subdued Sunlight	Mauve
	128		Warm	Effect	Middle Rose
103	129		Warm	Moderate Spread	Tough Frost
111	129		Neutral	Maximum Spread	Tough Rolux
00	130		Neutral		Clear
68	132	856	Cool	Effect, Cyc, Morning Sky Tones	Sky Blue
	134		Warm	Effect, Afternoon Sun	Golden Amber
	135		Warm	Effect, Afternoon Sun	Deep Golden Amber
	135		Warm	Cyc, Back Lighting	Deep Amber
	136	840	Neutral	Area, General Washes	Light Lavender
55	137	843	Neutral	Area, General Wash — Tinting	Special Lavender
88	138		Neutral	Effect, Sunny Spring Morning	Light Green
	141	856	Cool	Effect, Cyc, Morning Sky Tones	Sky Blue
	142		Cool	Effect, Evening Scenes	Pale Navy Blue
72	144		Cool	Area, Light Midday Sky	Azure Blue
17	147		Warm	Area, Tinting Washes	Light Flame

LUX	LEE	LENE	TEMP	COMMON USES	DESCRIPTION
18	147	811	Warm	Effect, Afternoon Sun	Flame
46	148		Warm	Toning, Background & Set Wash	Magenta
	151		Warm	Area, Sunrise	Gold Tint
	152	803	Warm	Area, Natural Sunlight	Medium Bastard Amber
	153		Warm	Area, Good for Skin Tones	Pale Salmon
05	154		Warm	Area, Gives Skin "Rosy" Look	Rose Tint
99	156	882	Warm	Area, Warms/Reduces Intensity	Chocolate
32	157	830	Warm	Effect	Medium Salmon Pink
23	158	817	Warm	Effect, Romantic Sunlight	Orange
06	159	804	Warm	Area, Interiors	No Color Straw
67	161	852	Cool	Area, Cyc, Excellent Sky Color	Light Sky Blue
02	162	803	Warm	Area, Enhances Skin Tones	Bastard Amber
19	164		Warm	Special Effect, Fire	Fire
25	164	818	Warm	Effect, Sunlight	Orange Red
67	165	851	Cool	Area, Cyc, Excellent Sky Color	Light Sky Blue
	166		Warm	Effect	Medium Salmon Pink
52	170	840	Neutral	Area, General Washes	Light Lavender
64	174		Cool	Area, Realistic Moonlight	Light Steel Blue
01	176	802	Warm	Area, Strong Sunlight	Light Bastard Amber
30	176		Warm	Area, Warm Skin Tones	Light Salmon Pink
	179		Warm	Effect, Candle/Fire	Deep Straw
	180		Cool	Cyc, Effect, Deep Night	Dark Lavender
59	181		Warm	Effect, Cyc, Bold Washes	Indigo
26	182	819	Warm	Sunlight, Near Primary	Light Red
	183	858	Cool	Effect, Cyc, Moonlight	Brilliant Blue
	192		Warm	Effect, Bright Musicals	Flesh Pink
32	193		Warm	Effect	Rosy Amber
	194		Neutral	Area	Surprise Pink
83	195	863	Cool	Cyc, Non-Realistic Night Sky	Medium Blue
65	196		Cool	Area, Dull Sky, Somber Moods	Daylight Blue
82	197		Cool	Effect	Surprise Blue
60	202		Cool	Area	No Color Blue

LUX	LEE	LENE	TEMP	COMMON USES	DESCRIPTION
97	209	880	Neutral	Reduce Color Brightness 1 Stop	Light Grey
98	210		Neutral	Reduce Color Brightness 2 Stops	Medium Grey
105	214		Neutral	Minimum Spread, Reduced Intensity	Tough Spun
106	215		Neutral	Minimum Spread, Reduced Intensity	Light Tough Spun
103	216		Warm	Moderate Spread	Tough Frost
108	224		Cool	Moderate Spread	Daylight Frost
104	228		Neutral	Moderate Spread One Direction	Tough Silk
33	248		Warm	Area, Bright — Musicals	No Color Pink
102	250		Warm	Moderate Spread	Light Tough Frost
101	253		Neutral	Minimum Spread	Light Frost
114	253		Neutral	Lightest Spread	Hamburg Frost

7. Troubleshooting Guide

CONDITION	POSSIBLE COURSE OF ACTION
Fixture won't light	
• Other fixtures in circuit okay	Start at fixture and check for - lamp failure - cable or connector failure - fixture wiring failure
• All other fixtures on circuit also have problem; other fixtures on dimmer okay	Start check at dimmer output for - connector failure - cable failure
• All fixtures on dimmer have problem	Start check at dimmer for - dimmer failure If dimmer checks out okay, move toward front end (control board) and check for - control cable failure - control board failure
Fixture flickers or flashes	
• Other fixtures in circuit okay	Check at fixture for - inadequate or loose plug connection - improper seating of lamp - loose fixture or connector wiring
• All other fixtures on circuit also have problem; other fixtures on dimmer okay	Check at dimmer output for - inadequate or loose plug connection - loose wiring
• All fixtures on dimmer have problem	Check at dimmer output for - inadequate or loose plug connection - loose wiring - improper connection of control cable Check at control board for - improper connection of control cable - dirty or defective potentiometer

Fixtures on dimmer won't turn off	Check at dimmer for - dimmer failure If dimmer checks out okay, check at control board for - control board failure
Fixtures on dimmer "ghost"	Check at dimmer for - improper adjustment (trim) If dimmer checks out okay, check at control board for - dirty or defective potentiometer
Fixtures on dimmer begin fade up, then bump to full before pot is at full	Check at dimmer for - improper adjustment (trim) If dimmer checks out okay, check at control board for - dirty or defective potentiometer
Fixtures on dimmer begin fade down, then black out before pot is off	Check at dimmer for - improper adjustment (trim) If dimmer checks out okay, check at control board for - dirty or defective potentiometer
Fixtures on dimmer won't reach full intensity	Check at dimmer for - improper adjustment (trim) If dimmer checks out okay, check at control board for - dirty or defective potentiometer

Procedures for Checking Failure

Keep in mind that the fastest way to determine whether an item is bad is to replace it with a like item known to be good. If the problem is rectified, you can feel confident that the part replaced was bad. Substitution with known good components is the most positive testing method available.

Lamp failure

- Before opening a fixture, testing the unit at the connector using a continuity tester or VOM set for ohms or resistance readings can indicate if the lamp is good. If the meter indicates a complete circuit (read the instructions with your meter), the lamp should be good and the problem is probably not within the fixture.
- Testing the lamp across its contacts with a continuity tester (or VOM) should indicate whether it is good or not.
- Often a lamp will fail due to being improperly or only partially seated in the lamp socket.

Cable and connector failure

- Testing across the contacts of each end of a free cable with a continuity tester or VOM should indicate if the cable is good.
- If there is power at one end of the cable and no power at the other, the cable is likely to be the problem.

- A loose connection within a connector can cause failure, often intermittently.
- With stage pin connectors (2P&G) the pin occasionally needs to be spread at the slit in the male plug to ensure adequate contact. Press a sharp blade into the slit; be sure the blade is not too thick or it will snap the pin in half.

Dimmer failure

Other than changing a fuse or resetting a circuit breaker, most dimmer failures should be handled only by trained technicians.

- The first thing to check when a dimmer fails is the fuse or circuit breaker.
- Always be sure the dimmer has not inadvertently been given a load larger than its maximum rating (overloaded).
- A loose control cable can cause many different conditions to occur, often intermittently.
- Using a volt meter to check output of a dimmer (200V AC range) or control cable (12V DC range) should indicate the condition of the unit. Be sure to keep some load on the dimmer when testing it. Some dimmers will read an output voltage even if the control board is off if there is no load on them.

Control board failure

Most problems occurring with a control board demand the attention of a trained technician.

- The first thing to check when a problem leads to the control board is the control cable. It can work loose and is the easiest part to replace.
- Periodic cleaning of any slider pots with a contact cleaner (check with your board manufacturer for which to use) will keep dust and grime from hurting their performance.

8. Useful Addresses

Altman Stage Lighting
57 Alexander Street
Yonkers, NY 10701
914-476-7987
Fixtures

Betterway Books
1507 Dana Avenue
Cincinnati, OH 45207
513-531-2222, 800-289-0963
Theater crafts/performing arts books

Broadway Press
120 Duane Street, Suite 407
New York, NY 10007
212-693-0570
Theater books

Drama Book Shop
723 Seventh Avenue
New York, NY 10019
212-944-0595
Theater bookstore

Educational Theatre Association
3368 Central Parkway
Cicinnati, OH 45225-2392
513-559-1996
Association for students and teachers

Electronic Theatre Controls
3002 Laura Lane
Middleton, WI 53562
608-831-4116
Control

Electronics Diversified, Inc.
1675 NW 218th Avenue
Hillsboro, OR 97124
503-645-5533
Control

The Fireside Theatre
6550 East 30th Street
P.O. Box 6372
Indianapolis, IN 46206-6372
Theatre book club

General Electric Lighting
Nelsa Park
East Cleveland, OH 44112
216-266-2121, 800-626-2000
Lamps

Great American Market
826 N. Cole Avenue
Hollywood, CA 90038
213-461-0200
Patterns, effects, color media

Kliegl Bros.
5 Arial Way
Syosset, NY 11791
516-937-3900
Control

Lee Colortran
1015 Chestnut Street
Burbank, CA 91506
818-843-1200
Fixtures, control, color media

Leprecon/CAE
10087 Industrial Drive
Hamburg, MI 48139
313-231-9373
Control

Lighting & Electronics
Market Street Industrial Park
Wappingers Falls, NY 12590
914-297-1244
Fixtures

Lighting Associates
P.O. Box 299
Chester, CT 06412
203-526-9315
Lighting drafting templates

Lighting Dimensions
135 Fifth Avenue
New York, NY 10010
212-677-5997
Theater publication

Lycian Stage Lighting
Kings Highway
Sugar Loaf, NY 10981
914-469-2285
Followspots

North American Philips Lighting
Philips Square
Somerset, NJ 08873
201-563-3000
Lamps

Osram Sylvania
18725 North Union Street
Westfield, IN 46074
800-762-7191
Lamps

Phoebus Manufacturing
2800 Third Street
San Francisco, CA 94107
415-550-1177
Followspots

Rosco
36 Bush Avenue
Port Chester, NY 10573
914-937-1300
Color media, patterns

Strand Lighting
18111 S. Santa Fe Avenue
Rancho Dominguez, A 90224
213-632-5519
Fixtures, control

Strong International
4350 McKinley Street
Omaha, NE 68112
402-453-4444
Followspots

Theatre Crafts
135 Fifth Avenue
New York, NY 10010
212-677-5997
Theater publication

Theatre Magic
6099 Godown Road
Columbus, OH 43235
614-459-3222
Effects, patterns

Thorn EMI
L.E. Nelson Sales Corp.
20 Bushes Lane
Elmwood Park, NJ 07407
Lamps

Ushio America, Inc.
20101 South Vermont Avenue
Torrance, CA 90502
213-329-1960
Lamps

USITT
10 West 19th Street
New York, NY 10011
212-924-9088
Theatrical trade organization

Venture Lighting
625 Golden Oak Parkway
Cleveland, OH 44146
800-338-6161
Lamps

9. Math for the Lighting Designer

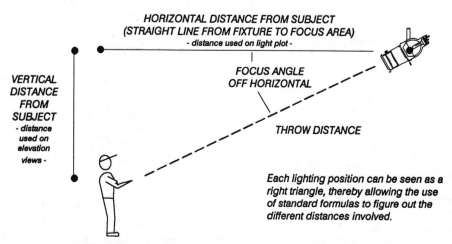

HORIZONTAL DISTANCE FROM SUBJECT
(STRAIGHT LINE FROM FIXTURE TO FOCUS AREA)
- distance used on light plot -

FOCUS ANGLE
OFF HORIZONTAL

VERTICAL DISTANCE FROM SUBJECT
- distance used on elevation views -

THROW DISTANCE

Each lighting position can be seen as a right triangle, thereby allowing the use of standard formulas to figure out the different distances involved.

Throw Distance = SQUARE ROOT[(vertical height)² + (horizontal distance)²]

Throw Distance = horizontal distance / COS(focus angle off horizontal)

Throw Distance = vertical height / SIN(focus angle off horizontal)

Horizontal Distance = SQUARE ROOT[(throw distance)² - (vertical height)²]

Horizontal Distance = vertical height / TAN(focus angle off horizontal)

Horizontal Distance = throw distance x COS(focus angle off horizontal)

Vertical Height = SQUARE ROOT [(throw distance)² - (horizontal distance)²]

Vertical Height = horizontal distance x TAN(focus angle off horizontal)

Vertical Height = throw distance x SIN(focus angle off horizontal)

Focus Angle Off Horizontal = ATAN(vertical height / horizontal distance)

Focus Angle Off Horizontal = ASIN(vertical height / throw distance)

Focus Angle Off Horizontal = 90° - ASIN(horizontal distance / throw distance)

Other useful formulas:

Beam Angle Multiplying Factor = 2 x TAN(Beam Angle / 2)

Beam Angle = 2 x ATAN(Beam Angle Multiplying Factor / 2)

Beam spread = Throw Distance x Beam Angle Multiplying Factor

Throw Distance = Beam Spread / Beam Angle Multiplying Factor

Beam Angle Multiplying Factor = Beam Spread / Throw Distance

Footcandles = Candlepower / (Throw Distance)²

Candlepower = Footcandles x (Throw Distance)²

Throw Distance = SQUARE ROOT[Candlepower / Footcandles]

Watts = Volts x Amps

Amps = Watts / Volts

Index